Ethel Waters

Stormy Weather

Stephen Bourne

THE SCARECROW PRESS, INC.
Lanham, Maryland • Toronto • Plymouth, UK
2007

SCARECROW PRESS, INC.

Published in the United States of America
by Scarecrow Press, Inc.
A wholly owned subsidiary of
The Rowman & Littlefield Publishing Group, Inc.
4501 Forbes Boulevard, Suite 200, Lanham, Maryland 20706
www.scarecrowpress.com

Estover Road
Plymouth PL6 7PY
United Kingdom

British Library Cataloguing in Publication Information Available

Library of Congress Cataloging-in-Publication Data

Bourne, Stephen, 1957 Oct. 31–
  Ethel Waters : Stormy weather / Stephen Bourne.
    p. cm.
  Includes bibliographical references and index.
  ISBN-13: 978-0-8108-5902-9 (pbk. : alk. paper)
  ISBN-10: 0-8108-5902-5 (pbk. : alk. paper)
  1. Waters, Ethel, 1896-1977. 2. Singers—United States—Biography. I. Title.

ML420.W24B68 2007
782.42164092—dc22
[B]   2006037121

∞™ The paper used in this publication meets the minimum requirements of
American National Standard for Information Sciences—Permanence of Paper
for Printed Library Materials, ANSI/NISO Z39.48-1992.
Manufactured in the United States of America.

~

Contents

~

Acknowledgments

I would like to thank the following for their help and friendship: Steven Cap-
suto, Randall Cherry, Bill Egan, Ray Funk, James Gavin, Keith Howes,
Delilah Jackson, Gail Lumet Buckley, Professor Edward Mapp, Deborah
Montgomerie, Joan Nestle, Hugh Palmer, Ken Sephton, Aaron Smith,
Robert Taylor, and Lydia Waters Thomas. All the photographs in this book
come from the author's private collection. The two portraits by Albert
Leonard have been reproduced with his permission.

I would also like to thank the New York Public Library, particularly the
Schomburg Center for Research in Black Culture and the Library for the
Performing Arts at Lincoln Center; the British Film Institute; and the
British Library.

The extract from Langston Hughes's *The Man Who Went to War* has been
reprinted with the permission of Harold Ober Associates Incorporated (copyright 1944 by Langston Hughes). The transcript of *Woman's Hour* in appendix B has been included with permission from the BBC, Jenni Murray, and
Radio 4.

Though every care has been taken, if we have included any copyright material without acknowledgment or permission, through inadvertence or fail-
ure to trace the present owners, we offer our apologies to all concerned.

This book is dedicated to the memory of my friend, actress and singer
Joanne Campbell (1964–2002), who was so wonderful as Josephine Baker in
This Is My Dream at the Theatre Royal, Stratford East, in 1986, and as Mil-
lie Gibson, a character based on Ethel Waters, in *The Cotton Club* at the

Aldwych Theatre in 1992. In 1993 we were interviewed about Ethel Waters by Jenni Murray on BBC Radio 4's *Woman's Hour* (see appendix B), and in 1997 Joanne impersonated Ethel in *Sophisticated Ladies*, a tribute to black women in British music and musical theatre from the 1850s to the 1950s, which I researched and scripted for BBC Radio 2.

Introduction

I sing because I'm happy,
I sing because I'm free,
For His eye is on the sparrow,
And I know He watches me.[1]

The opening of Ethel Waters's autobiography, *His Eye Is on the Sparrow*, published in 1951, is shocking: "I never was a child. I never was coddled, or liked, or understood by my family. I never felt I belonged. I was always an outsider."[2] Though Ethel overcame her disadvantaged childhood to become the most famous African American actress, singer, and entertainer of her time, since her passing in 1977 she has been "written out" of most published histories of jazz, popular music, cinema, and theatre. For the last thirty years, Ethel the innovator, trailblazer, and charismatic star loved by millions has been an outsider once again.

For example, when David Thomson compiled his *New Biographical Dictionary of Film* in 2002, in spite of it's being the fourth edition, revised and updated, with 1,300 entries (including 300 new entries), Ethel was missing again, and yet she was one of the first black women to play starring roles in American cinema. When I questioned Thomson about his exclusion of Ethel and several other notable African American film actresses, including Josephine Baker, Lena Horne, and Cicely Tyson, he replied, "I sympathize with you. In compiling the *Dictionary*, I come under a lot of pressure to include more of this and more of that—more of Iran, Japan, and so on. But there are plain limits to how big the book can be. Still, to take your questions in order: yes, Horne and Waters, at least, should be there."[3]

However, it isn't just white historians who have overlooked Ethel Waters. In 1991 four African American women coauthored *Book of Black Heroes, Volume Two: Great Women in the Struggle*. The book, aimed at young readers, features short essays about nearly one hundred African American women who helped shape American history. I do not wish to embarrass the authors by naming them, for this is a useful book, but they should have included Ethel in their Performing Artists section with, among others, Marian Anderson, Katherine Dunham, Mahalia Jackson, Lena Horne, Ella Fitzgerald, Leontyne Price, Miriam Makeba, Cicely Tyson, and Aretha Franklin. This is harsh treatment for a majestic African American woman who, at the height of her career in the 1930s, 1940s, and early 1950s, was a fascinating combination of strength, power, and refinement.

In the 1950s and 1960s, Ethel found herself out of step with other African Americans because she didn't take part in the civil rights movement. She didn't join hands with Dr. Martin Luther King, or take to the streets in protest marches, or make speeches. She rejected the term *black*: "We are many colours. Nobody in our race is jet black. It is something that originated way back when Marcus Garvey wanted to get us to Africa. I'm a brown-skinned woman. If you call me negro, I'm a nationality. If you call me nigger, I'm gonna hit you in the mouth, and you know I'm a Christian. And I feel the same way if you call me black. I just don't buy it."[4] This set her apart from other African Americans, and some of them looked on her as a relic from the bad old days, an "Uncle Tom." As a follower of Jesus, especially after 1957 when she dedicated her life to Him, Ethel became involved in a *white* religious movement. Her involvement with Billy Graham's crusades meant that her remarkable achievements from the 1920s to the 1950s, both as an entertainer and as an African American trailblazer, were ignored, forgotten, and erased from the history books. It is hoped that this modest tribute will help put the record straight.

Ethel Reappraised

Around 1918, a young Ethel, struggling on the road at the dawn of her singing and acting career, appeared at the 91 Theatre in Atlanta on the same bill as Bessie Smith, otherwise known as the Empress of the Blues. Bessie is generally considered to be the greatest blues singer of all, and her big-hearted, no-nonsense style was in tune with the mood of the "Jazz Age." The Empress was also tough on any singer she thought might be a possible threat. On this occasion, she laid down the law, insisting Ethel could not sing any blues onstage. But Ethel, though she sang with an air of refinement in an era of "blues shouters," was not so easily cowed by the older woman. During her act, when the audience cried out for Ethel to sing the blues, she broke Bessie's rule.

Years later, Ethel recalled what happened when Bessie confronted her after the performance. "You ain't so bad," said the Empress. "It's only that I never dreamed that anyone would be able to do this to me in my own territory and with my own people."[5]

Though the Empress did cross over into the white mainstream, she remained firmly a part of the African American community. Others—Ethel, Adelaide Hall, Josephine Baker, Billie Holiday, and Ella Fitzgerald—began here also but eventually became just as popular with white audiences. And it was Ethel, forgotten today when Bessie, Billie, and Ella are as popular as ever, who initially went on to make the most of this kind of success.

From the beginning, Ethel seemed to buck trends. Her public debut was around 1917, when blues women such as Ma Rainey and Bessie Smith were well established—but her first recordings (she debuted with "The New York Glide" on Cardinal Records, March 21, 1921) predate theirs. According to Sally Placksin, "Waters recorded throughout the twenties, producing hit after hit. Whatever she sang, she sang with dignity and authority, and her voice, her diction, her phrasing, her persona changed to suit each song. She sang her songs, and on occasion, as she herself said, she recited them; always the sense of drama and intimacy was implicit in her shaping of the material. . . . She brought to the blues a new sophistication and class."[6]

Ethel not only transformed such songs as "Dinah," "Am I Blue?" "Stormy Weather," and Irving Berlin's "Heat Wave" into classics but also, almost single-handedly, faced down the myth that black women could perform only as singers. Having triumphed in black vaudeville and theatre revues, in the mid-1920s she moved over to what was known as "white time." She was one of the first black performers to do so, and she was almost immediately acclaimed by white critics and audiences alike. Establishing herself as one of America's highest-paid entertainers, she began to look for dramatic roles, and she found them. Tough, uncompromising, courageous, and ambitious, she became one of the first African American women to be given equal billing with white stars on the Broadway stage and—when some of these productions were made into Hollywood films—to play leading on-screen roles.

She may have pioneered a more sophisticated style of jazz and blues singing, but she was no soft touch. She suffered an unhappy childhood, failed relationships, racism. This is, after all, a woman who believed she was conceived when her mother was raped at the age of twelve, a woman who, as a child, was running with the street gangs in Chester, Pennsylvania. In the world of white show business she always felt herself an outsider—and she was not afraid to make white audiences feel uneasy. In Irving Berlin's Broadway revue *As Thousands Cheer* (1933), she sang "Supper Time." In her words, "It told the story of a colored woman preparing the evening meal for her husband who had been lynched. If one song can tell the whole tragic history of a race, 'Supper Time' was that song. In singing it I was telling my comfortable, well-fed, well-dressed listeners about my people . . . those who had been slaves and those who were now downtrodden and oppressed."[7] When she introduced the famous torch song "Stormy Weather" at Harlem's Cotton Club that same year, she described it as the theme song of her life.

For years black womanhood was marginalized in Hollywood films, reduced to a simple comic stereotype: the bandanna-wearing mammy on Southern plantations. However, in 1943, top-billed Ethel gave an unforgettable performance in MGM's *Cabin in the Sky*, a stylish, almost surreal musical fantasy, which also featured Rochester, Lena Horne, Louis Armstrong, and Duke Ellington. Ethel stole the show, especially when she sang "Taking a Chance on Love." This was a personal triumph, but it cut short her Hollywood career, as she later explains: "There was conflict between the studio and me from the beginning. . . . I won all my battles on that picture. But like many other performers, I was to discover that winning arguments in Hollywood is costly."[8] However, Ethel was the first genuine black female movie star in America and the first black actress to receive top billing in films. A few years later, in the early 1950s, as the earth-mother Berenice in the stage and screen versions of *The Member of the Wedding*, Ethel made an impact in a complex dramatic role. With her portrayal, she buried forever the one-dimensional image of the one-dimensional mammy. Twenty years later, in writing about Ethel in the film version of *The Member of the Wedding*, African American film historian Donald Bogle noted the following:

> She emerged now as more than just a representative of the long-suffering, strong black woman. She was a great "serious" popular myth come true. For black audiences, Ethel Waters was the personification of the black spirit they believed had prevailed during the hard times of slavery, and they felt she brought dignity and wisdom to the race. For the mass white audience, Ethel Waters spoke to an inner spirit of a paranoid and emotionally paralyzed generation that longed for some sign of heroism. Movie stardom itself has often been based on a thin line between actress and myth, and with this performance Ethel Waters became a genuine movie star. Her personality, rather than her character or her movie, had grasped the public imagination, and thus the history of the Negro in American films gained a new perspective.[9]

In the late 1950s, ill health forced Ethel into semi-retirement, and she passed away in 1977 at the age of eighty. Deeply religious, in 1957 she gave up show business for Jesus. Most of her latter-day public appearances were made with Billy Graham's evangelical rallies. Though her voice gradually deteriorated, it still held audiences spellbound, whether singing "His Eye Is on the Sparrow" at Billy Graham rallies or making occasional guest appearances on television. She reminded the American public of the giant she once was and of the singer who had inspired and influenced countless singers who came after her.

In the 1980s, jazz musician Garvin Bushell observed that Ethel had turned out to be an important influence: "Mildred Bailey had some of her style, Lena Horne has a lot, and there were others. I'd say the three major influences in jazz singing have been Ethel, Louis Armstrong and Billie Holiday. Ethel always had great diction; you could hear every word. You see where Lena Horne got her style from?"[10] In 1958 Frank Sinatra acknowledged that, as a youngster, he had paid close attention to black jazz musicians such as Louis Armstrong and Duke Ellington and singers such as Ethel: "When I was a youngster struggling to find myself, I heard a lot of Ethel Waters, whose feeling for the blues and great warmth touched me deep down. I shall never forget her."[11] Sinatra did not forget Ethel or the debt he owed her. On the occasion of her eightieth birthday in 1976, he sent her a letter of congratulations and signed it, affectionately, "Francis Albert." Judy Garland acknowledged that Ethel's singing had moved her.[12] However, the most important tribute came from gospel singer Mahalia Jackson. She said that, without Ethel, there would not have been Billie Holiday, Lena Horne, Sarah Vaughan, Ella Fitzgerald, and Mahalia herself. They all acknowledged Ethel as their pioneer.[13] However, if this is true, apart from Mahalia, these great ladies of song acknowledged Ethel's influence in private, for as Holiday's biographer Donald Clarke points out, "Ethel Waters has been described as a 'rotten bitch, she hated and resented everybody,' which is why although 'Lady, Lena, Dinah [Washington], Sarah, all of them got something from Ethel, they never gave her any credit.'"[14] Cornetist Jimmy McPartland remembers: "We [Bix Beiderbecke and the Austin High Gang] liked Bessie Smith very much too, but Waters had more polish. . . . She phrased so wonderfully, the natural quality of her voice was so fine, and she sang the way she felt."[15] Bruce Crowther and Mike Pinfold acknowledge that, "of the three major jazz voices of the 1920s, Bessie Smith, Louis Armstrong and Ethel Waters, it is the latter who must be regarded as the most influential of all. Bessie Smith is the yardstick by which all blues singers are measured; Louis Armstrong, the innovator, created a style and was *the* original jazz voice; but Ethel

Waters transcended most positively and effectively the wider boundaries of American popular song. . . . It was Waters, even more so than Armstrong, who demonstrated that jazz style was adaptable to popular song."[16]

Ethel Waters possessed wide-ranging talent, and perhaps with the exception of Paul Robeson and Bill "Bojangles" Robinson, at the peak of her fame and popularity, no other black star was held in such affectionate high regard. She brought much of the startlingly innovative and subtle character of black theatre in the 1920s (the era of the Harlem Renaissance) into the mainstream, and even into Broadway and Hollywood. Sadly, although she is arguably the most influential woman blues and jazz singer of the 1920s and 1930s, and a major black figure in twentieth-century theatre, cinema, radio, and television, she is now the least remembered.

Move Over Doris Day

I have always been drawn to singers of popular songs because I want to hear the words, the story, which has been put to music. When Ella Fitzgerald sings something by Cole Porter or Rodgers and Hart, it is something to be enjoyed and cherished. Ella is often referred to as the First Lady of Song, and who am I to challenge that? But Ella is not *my* first lady; I've been listening to Ethel since I was ten years old, and to my ears *she* is the greatest. Ella can be a joy to listen to, but she doesn't touch my soul. Ethel does, and I agree with those who have described her as an actress who dramatizes the lyrics to her songs. With a torch song such as "Stormy Weather," she inhabits a character and acts out the drama in Ted Koehler's lyric. This is what draws me to Ethel the singer.

I can identify exactly when my interest in Ethel began. It was 1968. I was ten years old, and on television every Wednesday evening was a long-running series called *The Hollywood Musical*. According to the BBC's television and radio listings magazine *Radio Times*, this included "musical milestones from the golden days of the silver screen." Every Wednesday evening my father went out to a darts match in a local public house, and my mother allowed my sister and me to stay up later than usual (even though we had to go to school the next day). This had nothing to do with my father being strict or anything, it just happened that way. I loved films. I come from a working-class background, and films that I saw at the cinema and on television provided me with a form of escapism from the inner-city environment in which I grew up. As a youngster in the 1960s, I was lucky. I was part of the generation that saw Julie Andrews in *Mary Poppins* and *The Sound of Music* for the first time on a cinema screen, not theatrical, video, or DVD reissues. Walt Disney films were always being released or reissued, and so the films I found myself exposed to were, for the most part, innocent family escapist entertainment. And so, on June 19, 1968, in the Hollywood musical series, I watched *Cabin in the Sky*, and to this day I can still remember how it mesmerized me. The cast featured the lovely Lena Horne, gravel-voiced Eddie "Rochester" Anderson, jazz giants Louis Armstrong and Duke Ellington, and the dizzy waif Butterfly McQueen, but I was completely blown away by the star of the film, Ethel Waters. She was fabulous, and that was the turning point. That event in my life opened the door.

Any black actors I had seen in old Hollywood movies played servants. In *Cabin in the Sky*, the black characters had lives of their own. Ethel, Rochester, and Lena were the stars of the picture, not supporting players, and they played characters who were removed from the one-dimensional servant stereotypes. Unlike their white contemporaries, I sensed something different about them. They seemed real. At that time, Doris Day was a great favorite of mine. She was fun, and she sang beautifully. Her old movies were always being revived on television. I'd seen her in musicals such as *By the Light of the Silvery Moon*, *Calamity Jane*, and *The Pajama Game* as well as comedies such as *Pillow Talk* with Rock Hudson. In the mid-1960s she was *still* a big star and appearing in films at my local cinema. So I could see Doris in lighthearted comedy capers such as *The Glass Bottom Boat* and *Caprice*. I heard her singing on the radio. Favorites such as "Secret Love" and "Move Over Darling" were always being played. I read about her in old movie magazines I picked up at a local secondhand magazine shop. She was on the cover of most of them! Always happy and smiling, Doris Day was the whitest film star you could imagine. She *was* the girl you wanted to have living next door even if, in the 1960s, she was no longer a girl, but nearly fifty!

However, as appealing as she was, Doris Day wasn't *real*. From my childhood point of view, Ethel *was* real. She stood out in the artificial world of an old black and white MGM musical. She had a strong, larger-than-life personality and sang straight from the heart, her voice full of feeling and emotion that stayed with you. There was nothing one-dimensional about Ethel (or Petunia Jackson, the character she played in *Cabin in the Sky*). Ethel forced me to sit up and take notice of her charismatic personality in a way that was startling. I had never experienced anything like this before. Move over Doris Day, my life was never the same again!

A few years later, America's Sweetheart Doris Day revealed a life as stormy as any diva's when she published her memoirs, *Doris Day: Her Own Story* (1975). Like Ethel, Doris had been through the mill, and her memoirs exposed the dark side of her lighter-than-air public persona. For love and trust Doris also turned to God, like Ethel, and to dogs. As I grew older I could see that

Doris was, like Ethel, staggeringly real in many of her films, especially *Storm Warning*, Alfred Hitchcock's *The Man Who Knew Too Much*, and *The Pajama Game*. So, as a young adult in the 1980s, I discovered that Doris was closer to Ethel than I could possibly have imagined when I was a child in the 1960s.

Discovering More about Ethel (and Lena)

As a youngster, the problem I faced soon became apparent. Though she re-tired from the big screen in 1968, there were at least two dozen Doris Day film revivals to be seen on television year after year, but only one Ethel Wa-ters movie: *Cabin in the Sky*. It took a few years for me to understand why this great artiste made so few film appearances. In the early 1970s, I discovered that both Ethel and her *Cabin in the Sky* costar, Lena Horne, had published autobiographies, and these were easy to access through interlibrary loans. Ethel's *His Eye Is on the Sparrow* and Lena's *Lena*, published in 1966, were revelations to me. I'd had no knowledge of the personal and professional struggles of the two stars of *Cabin in the Sky*. These two books gave me in-sights into their lives, and so did the 1970 reissue of Peter Noble's 1948 British publication, *The Negro in Films*, probably the first book ever published on the subject.

Then, in 1973, came the publication of Donald Bogle's groundbreaking study of black actors in Hollywood movies: *Toms, Coons, Mulattoes, Mammies and Bucks*. This book updated and extended Noble's pioneer work and taught me much more about Hattie McDaniel, Butterfly McQueen, Dorothy Dandridge, and a host of other important black women from the Golden Age of Hollywood. I still have the paperback of Bogle's book, the one I purchased as a teenager. It has been well read, and though frayed at the edges, it is one of my prized possessions. I owe a great deal to Donald Bogle. He featured Ethel not only in this book but also in subsequent books I purchased, each one a milestone and adding to my knowledge of her. These include *Brown Sugar: Eighty Years of America's Black Female Superstars* (1980), *Blacks in American Films and Television: An Illustrated Enyclopedia* (1988), *Primetime Blues: African Americans on Network Television* (2001), and *Bright Boulevards, Bold Dreams: The Story of Black Hollywood* (2005). Bogle also contributed an introduction to the 1992 Da Capo reissue of Ethel's autobiography.

After reading Bogle's pioneer book in 1973, I searched for, found, pur-chased, and read every book I could find on the subject that was published in that decade. A lot of American books were published on the subject at that time, and I managed to find all of them in London. They were mostly avail-able only in specialist bookshops, such as the popular Cinema Bookshop off

Tottenham Court Road, and I suspect there were probably only a handful of copies of each in the country, but I found them! I was looking! These included Ed Mapp's *Blacks in American Films: Today and Yesterday* (1971), Eileen Landay's *Black Film Stars* (1973), Daniel J. Leab's *From Sambo to Superspade: The Black Experience in Motion Pictures* (1975), Gary Null's *Black Hollywood* (1975), and Thomas Cripps's *Slow Fade to Black* (1977).

Ladies Sing the Blues

After reading Ethel's autobiography, the door opened for me to continue researching her life and career. Meanwhile, in 1973, Diana Ross's first film, *Lady Sings the Blues*, was released in Britain. I had known about Diana since early childhood, when I listened to her singing "Baby Love" with the Supremes on the radio. Diana was already established as a world famous pop star before she made this breakthrough in a film about jazz singer Billie Holiday. Diana was elevated to movie stardom on an international scale, the first black woman to achieve this since Dorothy Dandridge had starred in *Carmen Jones* in 1954. I enjoyed reading about Diana's movie debut and collected all the press clippings I could find in newspapers and film magazines. I bought the soundtrack album and, more important, the paperback reissue of Billie Holiday's autobiography. Of course it had a photo of Diana on the cover, to tie in with and promote the release of the movie, but reading Billie's painful story added to and extended my knowledge of black women in show business. In 1974, for a school examination, I was asked to read an extract from a book, and I chose the section in which Billie spoke about the terrible time she had in Hollywood when she was cast as a maid in the 1947 film *New Orleans*. However, musically Billie did not touch me in the way that Ethel did, though I found her autobiography very moving and painfully revealing about her difficult life. I discovered in jazz books and magazine articles that Billie and Ella were rated higher than Ethel. Billie is an acquired taste. She is someone highly regarded in the jazz world, and rightly so. Ella has a lovely voice, but she doesn't grab me in the way that Ethel does. I felt this as a teenager, and I still feel this today.

However, though Ethel was alive until I was nineteen, apart from *Cabin in the Sky* and a few films on television or at the National Film Theatre, she wasn't accessible in this country in the way that other legendary black women singers were, such as Ella, Lena Horne, and Eartha Kitt. For years Ella, Lena, and Eartha had been popular with British audiences, and they made many concert and television appearances in this country. In the 1970s, when I was a teenager, Ella, Lena, and Eartha were still visiting Britain and working here, and I searched for and collected everything I could find about them in newspapers and magazines. I also watched for them on television, usually in variety shows or old movies. When the compilation film *That's Entertainment!* was released in 1974, one afternoon I excused myself from school (without permission) and went to a grand cinema in London's West End to see it. I was too impatient to wait for the film to come to my local cinema on general release. Lena was featured singing "Honeysuckle Rose" with the great Benny Carter and his orchestra in *Thousands Cheer*, a film she had made for MGM in 1943, but her all-too-brief appearance was worth waiting for. I was spellbound. I couldn't afford to see Lena on stage until 1980, when she made a memorable appearance at the London Palladium, a sort-of trial run for her award-winning one-woman show *The Lady and Her Music*, which opened on Broadway the following year and came to London in 1984. Two years after the release of *That's Entertainment!*, a sequel was released called *That's Entertainment! Part 2*, and this featured Ethel singing "Taking a Chance on Love" in *Cabin in the Sky*.

Growing up in London, I was aware that we had two expatriate African American divas living here: Adelaide Hall and Elisabeth Welch. In the 1920s Adelaide and Elisabeth had both performed in black Broadway musicals, including the hit revue *Blackbirds of 1928*, which brought them to Paris in 1929. In the 1930s they both settled in London, and in 1935 a family connection to one of them occurred. My aunt Esther, a black Londoner born before the First World War, made dresses for Elisabeth. Aunt Esther continued making dresses for Elisabeth until 1941, when she left her job as a seamstress to undertake war work. In 1982 I saw Elisabeth for the first time in concert at the Riverside Studios in Hammersmith, and later that year she invited me to her beautiful home in Knightsbridge. We became friends, and in 2005, two years after she passed away at the age of ninety-nine, I published a biography, *Elisabeth Welch: Soft Lights and Sweet Music*.

I saw Adelaide in concert for the first time in 1983 and befriended her two years later after interviewing her about Francis Ford Coppola's film *The Cotton Club*. In 1989 I worked as a consultant on a documentary film about her life and career: *Sophisticated Lady*. Adelaide passed away in 1993, and eight years later I published a tribute—to commemorate her centenary—called *Sophisticated Lady: A Celebration of Adelaide Hall*. Both Adelaide and Elisabeth spoke highly of Ethel. For them, in the 1920s and 1930s, she was someone they looked up to: a trailblazer, an inspiration, and an important influence on their own singing styles.

In 1980 I made contact, by letter, with another black legend: Butterfly McQueen, famous for playing Scarlett O'Hara's hysterical servant Prissy in the movie classic *Gone with the Wind*. I found an address for her in *Who's Who in the Theatre*. Butterfly lived in New York, and I wrote to her. It was as simple as that. To my surprise—and delight—she replied! We never met, but we corresponded up to her death in 1995. As I had already guessed, I discovered that there was much more to her than playing a Hollywood stereotype. However, unlike Elisabeth and Adelaide, Butterfly did not have happy memories of Ethel (see chapter 10).

Discovering Ethel's Music and Movies

In the 1970s I discovered a marvelous record shop called 58 Dean Street Records, located in Soho, the heart of London's theatreland, between Oxford Street and Shaftesbury Avenue. It was there I discovered imports of American albums by artistes such as Ethel and Lena. The shop was small, cramped, and crammed with records, and it was always busy. Customers were always bumping into each other in their efforts to find their favorite singers. Of course Lena Horne was still recording in the 1970s, and I bought every new album she released from the major record shops. However, 58 Dean Street Records enabled me to discover the more obscure, hard-to-find titles. I didn't have much money in those days. I was still at school until 1977, and I worked only one day a week, on Saturdays, as a sales assistant in a shoe shop. But I saved my money, and when I could afford to, I would leave school and journey into London's West End to add to my collection of records and books. These excursions, which were adventures for the teenage lad from a southeast London council estate, filled me with excitement. Regarding Ethel, at 58 Dean Street Records, I purchased several imported compilation albums of her blues recordings and past hits including *Jazzin' Babies Blues: Ethel Waters 1921–27*; *Ethel Waters on Stage and Screen 1925–1940*; *Miss Ethel Waters* (a recording of a live performance in the late 1950s); *Cabin in the Sky* (movie soundtrack); and *Ethel Waters 1938–1939*, produced by Rosetta Reitz, whose reissues made it possible for many forgotten African American singers to be heard again. These recordings enabled me to hear, for the first time, Ethel's wonderful singing.

In 1974 I joined the National Film Theatre (also known as the NFT) in London, a repertory cinema that enabled me to see my film favorites. Naturally I gravitated toward Lena in MGM musicals, but membership in the NFT also gave me opportunities to see Ethel in some of the films she made after *Cabin in the Sky*, such as *Pinky* and *The Member of the Wedding*.

The Black Media

In the 1970s I was a fan and nothing more. I had no thoughts of *writing* about these great singing ladies of the screen. That didn't happen until the early 1980s. In the 1970s we, in Britain, didn't have the black media that America had. So even if I had wanted to write about Ethel, Lena, Eartha, and Miss Ross, there were no openings. We didn't have any mainstream black newspapers or magazines. We had the *Weekly Gleaner* imported from Jamaica, and one or two political journals published on shoestring budgets, but little else. The black media simply wasn't supported in this country.

Ebony, a glossy monthly lifestyle magazine aimed at African Americans, was imported from America, and I could buy it in Peckham, where I lived, because it was a multicultural area. *Ebony* was a revelation to me. In those days it had a large format, bigger than any British magazine. It contained wonderful, illustrated stories about some of my favorite stars, who were also featured on the covers: Lena, Miss Ross, Cicely Tyson, and many others. There were historical features, and it was here I began to read about African Americans from history including Sojourner Truth, Malcolm X, W. E. B. Du Bois, Martin Luther King, Harriet Tubman, and Mary McLeod Bethune. I was familiar with none of these people except Martin Luther King, whose assassination in 1968 made headlines around the world. *Ebony* gave me the opportunity to broaden my knowledge of African American history beyond *Gone with the Wind* and Paul Robeson, whom I *had* read about. *Ebony* had advertisements with good-looking African Americans advertising everything from cigarettes to the armed forces. In Britain, black models were not given that kind of exposure. In one edition of *Ebony*, Donald Bogle wrote a fantastic article about black humor in America, mentioning Stepin Fetchit, Hattie McDaniel, Redd Foxx, Moms Mabley, and Richard Pryor, and he placed them in a historical context, which was so useful. Reading issues of *Ebony* in the 1970s began to give me a historical context for Ethel and Lena.

It wasn't until the early 1980s that the situation began to change in Britain. That is when we started to publish glossy lifestyle magazines for black readers in this country, and I wrote for some of the early ones, such as *Root* and *Chic*. Others that I wrote for, such as *Staunch*, *Black Arts in London*, and *Artrage*, were more political and community based, but they had relatively short lives because of lack of funding and limited distribution. It was a well-known fact that, when sales of *Root* magazine began to fall, they'd put Diana Ross on the cover—sales would soar for that issue and help keep the publication going for a while longer! More often than not, there was nothing in the magazine about Miss Ross, it was just a ploy to boost their sales. And who could blame them? They were in competition with dozens of glossy lifestyle magazines aimed at white women, which swamped the market and were purchased by black women because there was nothing else on offer. And yet these white magazines *never* put black women on their covers. *Root* was one of the pioneers because it put beautiful black women on the covers and could be found on sale in areas of London with large black populations, such as Brixton, Notting Hill, and Peckham.

Writing for Black Journals

In the beginning, I had no training or experience. I was just an educationally disadvantaged kid from a working-class council estate in Peckham, but I had knowledge and enthusiasm. This early experience paid off, and in 1983 I was offered a place in a postgraduate course in journalism at the London College of Printing but I hadn't even graduated! I was the only student *without* a degree, and I was terrified. But I qualified because my work had been published in the black press, and this impressed the interviewer. The other students, almost without exception, were white middle-class graduates from some of the best universities in the country. So I had good reason to be proud of myself, especially when I passed the exams.

The journalism course included a one-week attachment to a magazine or newspaper. My fellow students chose to go to *The Guardian*, *The Observer*, *Financial Times*, or *Marie Claire*, but I chose *The Voice*, which had been successfully launched in 1982. This national weekly newspaper for black readers stood out from the others I had written for because it was properly distributed and sold *everywhere*. My time at *The Voice* was a success. The paper had good arts editors, who gave me lots of freelance work after I successfully completed my journalism course, but regrettably, in the early 1990s *The Voice* became a homophobic tabloid, and the quality of the writing suffered. The good arts editors they employed moved into television. So I stopped writing for them. However, in the 1980s, when I contributed to these journals, I was given the opportunity to write nostalgic tributes to *all* my favorites from the Golden Age of Hollywood: Lena Horne, Dorothy Dandridge, Hattie McDaniel, Dooley Wilson, Butterfly McQueen, Ethel Waters. I also conducted contemporary interviews with visitors to London, including Eartha Kitt when she appeared on the West End stage in *Follies*; director Robert Townsend when he came here to promote his film *Hollywood Shuffle*; and Lena Horne's daughter, Gail Lumet Buckley, at her London hotel when she came here to promote her book *The Hornes*. I interviewed her for a wonderful spread in *Chic* magazine, and though we haven't seen each other since, I've kept in touch with Gail, who—joy of joys—made it possible for me to acquire a signed photograph of her mother. I also broadened out into popular mainstream film journals. I remember writing an article about *The Color Purple* for *Films and Filming* and a lengthy, beautifully illustrated (from my personal collection) four-page spread about the history of black women in cinema (including Ethel) in *Photoplay*.

The National Film Theatre (NFT) and the BBC

I had already been a member of the NFT for ten years when I researched and programmed my first film season for them: the first retrospective of black British cinema (*Burning an Illusion*, June 1983). Shortly afterward, my proposal for an Ethel Waters retrospective was rejected by Sheila Whitaker, then head of program planning, but I never gave up hope of presenting this series. Some years later, this proposal was accepted after I resubmitted the idea, when Mark Adams replaced Sheila. *Ethel Waters: Stormy Weather* was presented in December 1993, and I am proud that I researched, devised, and put together the NFT's first tribute to a black female star in its (then) forty-year history. They'd honored just about every star from the Golden Age of Hollywood, including all the top female personalities: Bette Davis, Katharine Hepburn, Barbara Stanwyck, Joan Crawford, to name but a few, but in histories of Hollywood, Ethel had never been given the status she deserved, in spite of her leading roles in *Cabin in the Sky* and *The Member of the Wedding*. I was determined to give her that status at the NFT, and my tribute was a success, helping draw attention to this great artiste and her important contribution to popular cinema. Sadly, prints of some of her films were unavailable in Britain at that time, including *Gift of Gab* and *Stage Door Canteen*, but others were found in our National Film and Television Archive. A print of Ethel's first movie, *On with the Show!* (1929), was imported from the United States, and this rare screening (in Britain) drew the biggest audience. *The Member of the Wedding* drew the second largest audience. Afterward, an enthusiastic Mark Adams wrote to me: "Thank you very much for your contribution to our programme with the Ethel Waters season, now that the films have actually been on our screens. I think the season looked great in the booklet and I hope you are happy with the way the programme turned out." The publicity included a feature-length article I contributed to the jazz journal *Wire* as well as an interview on BBC Radio 4's *Woman's Hour* (for a transcript of this interview, see appendix B). I was joined by my friend, actress and singer Joanne Campbell, who had played a character based on Ethel in the West End stage musical *The Cotton Club* in 1992, and we were interviewed by Jenni Murray. The producer of the program, Ariane Koek, later wrote to me: "Thank you very much for all your help (and patience). It went very well and everyone said what a revelation Ethel was to them in the post mortem after the programme! So I think we all did our job! Joanne was great too and the clip from *Cabin in the Sky* was one which I love—completely mad when she says 'Good day, riff-raff'! Excellent fun. And as for the music . . . well I am still taping oodles of copies for everyone. So a fan club has most definitely formed." Clearly, Miss Waters made an impact at the BBC for the first time since her all-too-brief appearance on one of their radio shows in 1930 (see chapter 3).

After my appearance in *Woman's Hour*, for several years I featured Ethel Waters in radio programs I researched and scripted for the BBC Radio 2 network. These included *Star Equality* (1995), a tribute to black women in Hollywood musicals; *Sophisticated Ladies* (1997), a celebration of the lives and songs of a century of classy black divas, with extracts from their autobiographies read by Joanne Campbell; and *One Mo' Time* (1998), a tribute to the stars of black Broadway musicals. In 1998, I returned to the NFT to present an illustrated talk about Ethel in my *Black Women in Hollywood* series. Since then, it has been impossible to find outlets in Britain for my work on Ethel Waters.

Randall Cherry

In December 1993, during the run of my film season at the NFT, I met Randall Cherry, who shared my interest in—and enthusiasm for—the great lady. Randall was an African American student, at that time based in Paris, and we had fun comparing notes and sharing our research. Along with Donald Bogle, Randall belongs to a small group of Ethel Waters enthusiasts who have managed to publish work about her. I was overjoyed when Randall published not one but two superb reappraisals in collections of essays: "Ethel Waters: The Voice of an Era" in *Temples for Tomorrow: Looking Back at the Harlem Renaissance* (2001) and "Ethel Waters: Long, Lean, Lanky Mama" in *Nobody Knows Where the Blues Come From: Lyrics and History* (2005). Other exceptional works about Ethel include Henry Pleasants's chapter in *The Great American Popular Singers* (1974); Gary Giddins's 1977 essay "The Mother of Us All," reprinted in *Riding on a Blue Note: Jazz and American Pop* (1981); Susannah McCorkle's insightful appraisal of Ethel, also titled "The Mother of Us All," in *American Heritage* (1994); and Frank Cullen's appreciation in *Classic Images* (1996). Two books written by friends Ethel made during her Billy Graham years were published in 1978, shortly after her death: Juliann

DeKorte's *Finally Home* and Twila Knaack's *Ethel Waters: I Touched a Sparrow*. In addition to discovering these works, I have also continued to research and seek out material relating to Ethel and her career as a singer and actress, with an ever-growing collection of record albums, CDs, videos, and more recently, DVDs. I believe I have more than enough material to draw on for this book.

A Gay Perspective

To conclude, as a gay man, I want to try to understand—and come to terms with—my own appreciation of, and enthusiasm for, Ethel Waters. Does my sexuality have anything to do with why I have been drawn to this great but neglected and undervalued African American star? This is going to be a difficult exercise because so little work has been undertaken on why some gay men develop a strong identification with larger-than-life female stars.

I cannot ignore the fact that, as a teenager, when I read Ethel's autobiography, I related to her on the level of someone who felt educationally disadvantaged. However, it is also important to acknowledge that, in addition to being gay (an "outsider"), I am also white—from a biracial, working-class family—and my *cultural* identity has also drawn me to her (I was raised in an urban, culturally diverse part of London). All these experiences have informed my outlook on life and the perspective I take in my work.

In 1980, American writer Vito Russo explored gay men's appreciation of singer and actress Judy Garland in an edition of the British journal *Gay News*. Garland, who had passed away in 1969, had been a "gay icon" for several decades, and Russo's observations have proved helpful to my own understanding of my appreciation of Ethel Waters. According to Russo, "when you ask people what fascinated them about Judy Garland they usually use the word vulnerable. It was tremendously appealing, especially to gay people, that such an obviously strong woman could walk through fire and still appear vulnerable."[17] I can relate to that. Ethel was undoubtedly a strong woman who showed vulnerability. She was also, like Judy, a singer who sang from the heart without a hint of artifice. In this respect Ethel also bore similarities to her African American contemporary, Paul Robeson, whose warmth and sincerity "spoke" to millions. After she became famous, Ethel, like Judy Garland, lived out her private life in the public eye, and the highs and lows of her turbulent life were as dramatic and fascinating as Judy's. In the 1950s, after the stage and screen triumphs of *The Member of the Wedding*, Ethel's career fell apart, but like Judy, she seemed to be an iron butterfly who always came back.

When Russo made the following comment about Judy in performance, he could have been referring to Ethel. He said that Judy "always walked the thin line between triumph and terror. Her audience . . . was never sure whether she'd fall into the abyss or soar like a phoenix. One wanted to hold her and protect her because she was a lost lamb in a jungle, and yet be held by her and protected by her because she was a tower of strength, someone who had experienced hell but continued to sing about bluebirds and happiness. Nobody could be happy like Judy Garland, and yet beneath the quick wit and the hesitant laugh there was real horror. . . . Gays take chances all the time in ways straights never do. We have traditionally been forced to put on one face for the world and another in private."[18]

Notes

1. From *His Eye Is on the Sparrow*. Civilla D. Martin (words) and Charles H. Gabriel (music) (1905). Ethel Waters loved this hymn so much that she performed it in the stage and screen versions of *The Member of the Wedding* and used its name as the title of her autobiography.

2. Ethel Waters with Charles Samuels, *His Eye Is on the Sparrow* (New York: Da Capo, 1992), 1.

Note: All quotes and page references from *His Eye Is on the Sparrow* (Doubleday, 1951) are taken from the 1992 Da Capo edition.

3. Stephen Bourne, "How Black Actors and Filmmakers Have Fared in Film Encyclopaedias," *Black Filmmaker* 5, no. 19 (March/April 2003), 60.

4. Ethel Waters, *Just a Little Talk with Ethel*, a two-LP set released on the World Records label in 1977.

5. Waters, *Sparrow*, 92.

6. Sally Placksin, *Jazzwomen: 1900 to the Present* (London: Pluto Press, 1985), 26.

7. Waters, *Sparrow*, 222.

8. Waters, *Sparrow*, 258.

9. Donald Bogle, *Toms, Coons, Mulattoes, Mammies and Bucks: An Interpretive History of Blacks in American Films* (New York: Bantam, 1974), 232.

10. Garvin Bushell with Mark Tucker, *Jazz from the Beginning* (Oxford: Bayou Press, 1988), 32.

11. Frank Sinatra, "Jazz Has No Colour Bar!" *Melody Maker*, October 18, 1958, 3.

12. Anne Edwards, *Judy Garland* (London: Constable, 1975), 99.

13. Mahalia Jackson, from an interview in *Metronome*, December 1954, quoted in various sources including the sleeve notes to *Ethel Waters 1938–1939*, compiled by jazz historian Rosetta Reitz (Rosetta Records, 1986), and the commentary by film historian Kenneth Geist in the DVD release of *Pinky* (20th Century Fox Cinema Classics Collection, 2005).

14. Donald Clarke, *Wishing on the Moon: The Life and Times of Billie Holiday* (New York: Viking, 1994), 396.

15. Nat Hentoff and Nat Shapiro, eds., *Hear Me Talkin' to Ya: The Story of Jazz as Told by the Men Who Made It* (New York: Dover, 1978), 88.

16. Bruce Crowther and Mike Pinfold, *The Jazz Singers: From Ragtime to the New Wave* (Poole, U.K.: Blandford Press, 1986), 50–51.

17. Vito Russo, "Poor Judy," *Gay News* 205 (December 11–January 7 1980/1981), 14–15.

18. Russo, *Gay News*: 14–15.

Author's note: I have thoroughly enjoyed researching and writing this book, but it has been the most challenging project I have undertaken so far because it is so difficult to condense the breadth of Ethel's life and career. Readers expecting a definitive biography will be disappointed. This is intended to be an appraisal of her career—in particular her achievements as an actress—with an overview of her life. I focused on her theatrical career more than her music career because that is my primary area of interest. As I explained in this introduction, I am not an expert in blues and jazz. Where possible I have attempted to guide the reader to other sources.

CHAPTER ONE

~

I Never Was a Child

Ethel Waters was born on October 31, 1896 (not 1900 as stated in her 1951 autobiography), in Chester, Pennsylvania. The illegitimate child of Louise Anderson, Ethel claimed she had been conceived when her young mother was raped at knifepoint by John Waters. Louise was supposed to have been either twelve or thirteen years old (Ethel said twelve), and this has been reported in numerous books and articles about Ethel, but recent research undertaken by genealogist Deborah Montgomerie sheds new light on this story. Without Deborah's assistance, this chapter could not have been written. All the quotations from Ethel in this chapter are taken from *Just a Little Talk with Ethel*, a two-LP set released on the World Records label in 1977.

Louise is recorded in the 1880 United States Census as Louisa T. Anderson, age two. In various editions of *Who's Who in the Theatre*, Ethel entered her mother's name as Louisa Tar Anderson. On the Family Search website (www.familysearch.org), a Louisa Anderson is recorded who may well be Ethel's mother. She was born on December 7, 1877, in Philadelphia, the daughter of Lewis W. Anderson and Sallie. This indicates that she would have been eighteen when Ethel was born. In the 1900 census, Louise gave her date of birth as December 1877, but in other censuses the year is recorded as 1881. Several different years of birth appear in various censuses; however, this was usual with everyone in every country. The 1880 census is nearer the truth. She appears to have married only Norman Joseph Howard (born 1876), and she kept the name of Howard throughout her life. In the 1900 census, Louise and Norman are living in Pennsylvania with Ethel, whose birth date is recorded as October 1896.

Ethel's half sister, Genevieve, born June 29, 1898, was the only surviving child of Louise and Norman. The 1910 census says they had been married for thirteen years, which would have made 1897 the year of their marriage, shortly after Ethel was born. The 1910 census also shows that Louise mainly worked as a domestic and Norman as a laborer.

According to the 1880 census, Louise Anderson's household also included her father, Lewis Anderson, age forty-six, and he gave his occupation as "driver." Her mother, Sarah, age twenty-eight, was "keeping house." Louise's siblings are recorded as Viola, age seven; Charles, age five; and Edith, age two months.

In her autobiography, Ethel describes her grandfather "Louis" Anderson as one of the youngest drum majors in the Civil War. Further investigation by Deborah Montgomerie reveals that Lewis (Louis) was in the Civil War for a very short time. At the age of eighteen, Lewis B. Anderson enrolled as a musician (drummer) on September 13, 1862, serving on the Union side for the state of Pennsylvania, but "mustered out" due to an injury on September 28. Ethel also explains that Louis was not the father of the youngest child, Edith, who was nicknamed "Ching." With the exception of Sarah, whose birthplace is recorded as Delaware, all the family members were born in Pennsylvania. In 1880 they resided at 1447 Bronton Street in Pennsylvania.

Ethel always referred to her grandmother, Sarah, who died in 1914, as "Sally." For most of her childhood, Ethel was raised by Sally in Philadelphia: "My grandmother, whenever she could afford it, took care of me because my mother was only twelve years old, going on thirteen, when I was born. And then my mother later married my half-sister's father and my grandmother, Sally Anderson, clung to me, bless her heart. She worked hard all her life. She worked in service and she had three girls and one boy, and they were all young and wild, and there was no-one to care for them."

Ethel's father, John Waters, was born in March, 1878, which suggests he was around the same age as Louise when Ethel was conceived. In her autobiography, Ethel describes him as a playboy who worked as a pianist and was murdered (poisoned) in 1901 by a jealous lover. However, one of his granddaughters has given a different account to Deborah Montgomerie: "She says John was murdered but it was a tragic mistake. John was playing piano at a party, in a bar or club, and someone placed a drink that contained poison on the piano for someone else, but John drank it and died."

John was the son of William Waters, who was born in 1849 in Philadelphia and also died in 1901. He enlisted as a private in the Civil War in 1864 and was discharged the following year. He served in Company B, 25th U.S.

Colored Infantry. Most important, we learn from the Civil War records that William was a free man. His first wife, Mary, died in 1877. He married Ethel's grandmother, Lydia Timbers, in 1877 in Philadelphia. The 1880 census records that he was living as William Walters in Philadelphia with Lydia, two children from his first marriage, and John and Blanch from his second. Lydia and William actually had eight children in all, but only Harry lived to grow old.

Lydia was born on May 15, 1857, near Harpers Ferry, West Virginia, to James and Emily Ann Timbers. When Lydia was young, the family moved to Gettysburg, Pennsylvania, and at the age of twelve she moved to Camden, New Jersey, to live with an aunt. At about the age of fourteen, Lydia went into service, met William, and later married him. In her autobiography, Ethel describes her grandmother Lydia as Dutch, but she was not certain of her racial origins. Lydia's skin was "snowy white," but she could have been of African descent. Mixed marriages were illegal, so if Lydia was white, she could not have legally married Waters. Ethel never heard her spoken of as white, and she was accepted by her black neighbors as one of them. Her granddaughter, Lydia Waters Thomas, has explained to Deborah Montgomerie: "I think many members of the family had a rather fair complexion. The picture of Lydia as I remember it showed her to be very light. Either the picture has faded a great deal or I could see how people may have made incorrect assumptions about her race. Even the marriage license of my grandparents has large bold 'B's written over the 'W's in the line indicating 'color.' It was a mistake that clearly the clerk made and not them. They each signed the certificate and the hand writing is not the same for either of them." Lydia died sometime after 1914. She was alive and living in New Jersey when her son Harry married that year.

Ethel was born in poverty, and her 1951 autobiography reveals that she was rarely shown any love and affection. Raised in a vicious environment, she describes herself as a real dead-end kid and gang leader. To earn money as a child, she ran errands for pimps and prostitutes—many of the requests were for drugs. She also earned extra pennies as their lookout against the police. The "thieves' children" and "sporting women's trick babies" taught Ethel how to steal for food because she was always hungry. In elementary school, she distressed her teachers with her roughness and profanity.

On her mother's side, she was the product of a dysfunctional family. Some of the time she lived with her older alcoholic aunts (Vi and Ching), claiming she practically raised herself while living the life of a vagabond in the slums of Chester and Philadelphia. At a tender age, Ethel was exposed to the red-light districts where legal prostitution, gambling, and other vices were accepted as normal. There was very little stability in young Ethel's life, and so she became a thief, stealing food out of necessity:

> My aunts were just young girls. They weren't bad, but they were wild and they didn't care anything about how I was taken care of, so I had to fend for myself. Sometimes they'd forget to leave the key under the door and I had to sleep on the steps all night. My aunts had one tragic failure: they drank. And when they were sober they were the sweetest people on earth. But when they were high they took a certain almost hatred toward me because I couldn't stand the drinking. I knew what to expect when I'd see 'em. My aunts would fix the most beautiful meal in the world if they were sober and if they was on one of those binges—no food. But it was fun, we could sing.
>
> I got a pretty good education because anything went in the alley after dark, and I'm not talking about cats and dogs! So I knew all the answers and that protected me. I wasn't shy or demure or naïve. They thought I knew more than I did, but that was my protection. Believe me it *was* my protection [laughs]. I was a big shot, and I played it up. And being big for my age, I could pass for fifteen but I was really twelve and innocent, in every capacity.
>
> And another thing I want to get across. It wasn't segregated. It wasn't a coloured place. This place had different nationalities: Chinese, Italians, Negroes, Polish, Jewish. We were a melting pot. We all lived together. And when we kids went out on raids we went together and it wasn't to sell anything, it was to eat. So that way I got my schooling, in the school of life. I'm still attending. But, for me, the school of life began early. The trend of my life has been work earned by the sweat of your brow.
>
> Being the type of youngster I was, being large for almost as long as I can remember, it's helped me and hurt me too because I never had the chance of getting the love and the warmth and the affection that I so desperately wanted that a child gets, and any child that gets it he don't know how wonderfully blessed he is. I never had a shoulder to cry on and I never had a lap to sit on.

Occasionally, Ethel would be taken away by her mother and stepfather to their home in Chester. This happened when Louise came into conflict with Sally. When the young girl thought she was settled, Louise would take her away from her beloved grandmother. For years Ethel found herself at the center of a tug of love war between Louise and Sally:

> Whenever my mother would get mad at my blessed grandmother she knew one way to hurt her and that was to snatch me from her. I even tried to have myself put away because I was so tired of being shunted and shifted around. I adored Louise but she tolerated me. My aunts, Vi and Ching, and my grandmother, used to make fun of her religion but my mother was protestant in a dogmatic way about the Lord. I got a lot of that from her, because I like fire and

brimstone. Don't play around with me and my Lord. But, even though she was distant, I sensed the closeness. I always wanted to break down that thing. I felt that, if I could get to know her and she could get to know me, she'd like me better. That was a childish thought that I had. Louise left the bringing up to my grandmother but she would come and get me from Mom and take me to Chester to be with her and Pop Norman, but their reconciliations never lasted. I never wanted to go with her, but I couldn't say nothing.

Ethel was twelve years old when she found Jesus. "He touched me," she recalled, "And when you completely relinquish everything where Jesus is concerned, He takes over, a wave of something will come over you and, oh boy, you can't describe it, but you sense it, you feel it. And He let this twelve-year-old believe there was something. Then, when I went home, I wanted to hold it, I wanted to hug it. I didn't feel bad about things that hurt me from my childhood, how lonely I was, how lonesome I was. I wanted affection. And from Jesus I got something that I could cling to and, above all, I wasn't taking it from nobody else."

In the 1920 census, Louise was residing at 721 Fawn Street in Pennsylvania with her daughter Jennie (Genevieve), granddaughter Ethel Parker (age three), father Louis (age seventy-three), and sister Viola. Jennie gave her occupation as waitress.

In the 1930 census, Louise was residing at 1327 Catherine Street in Pennsylvania with her older sister Viola. Louise gave her age as forty-seven and her age at first marriage as fifteen. The two sisters gave their occupations as "housework (private family)."

According to the Family Search website, Louise Anderson (registered under her maiden name) died in 1962. It records her birthplace as Germantown, Pennsylvania, and the year of her birth as 1888 (not 1877 as recorded in the 1900 census). According to Ethel, she was living with her daughter Genevieve at the time of her death. Genevieve must have assumed Ethel was born in 1900—as stated in her 1951 autobiography—and believed her mother did give birth to Ethel at the age of twelve. Louise's parents are recorded as Lewis and Sally Anderson. Genevieve Howard's month and year of death are also recorded on the Family Search website. She passed away in January, 1987, in Pennsylvania at the age of eighty-eight. Howard was her maiden name. Ethel states in her 1972 autobiography that, after her mother's passing, Genevieve was her last surviving relative. When she passed away in 1987, Genevieve had survived her famous half sister by nine years. Finally, contrary to Ethel's autobiography, she did make peace with the Waters family and kept in contact with her uncle, Harry Waters, and his family for many years.

CHAPTER TWO

~

On with the Show!

Ethel never intended to go on the stage; her ambition was to become a maid and companion to a wealthy white woman who would travel the world—and take Ethel with her! She recalls in *Just a Little Talk with Ethel.* "When I worked in service, which I did constantly before I first went on the stage, I was a bus girl, chambermaid and waitress. When I had my Thursday off and went to get a meal, if the waitress gave me good service I'd bust a gut to give her a big tip I could ill afford because she had given me good service. I appreciate the little things people do for me."

Legend has it that on her birthday Ethel attended a Halloween party, where she was asked to sing. Listening to her were two vaudevillians, Braxton and Nugent, who invited her to join their act in Baltimore, Maryland, for two weeks. Ethel accepted and teamed up with the Hill Sisters, Maggie and Jo. They named her Sweet Mama Stringbean because she was so scrawny and tall. For her stage debut, Ethel wanted to sing "St. Louis Blues," W. C. Handy's popular blues song. It was a number she had heard performed by a female impersonator called Charles Anderson. So Ethel wrote to the song's copyright owners, Harry H. Pace and Handy, for permission, which they granted. "St. Louis Blues," one of the most durable and popular blues songs ever written, helped establish Ethel. In fact, Ethel became the first woman to publicly perform the classic song. According to Handy, he was inspired to write it while wandering the streets of St. Louis. He met a black woman tormented by her husband's absence, and she told Handy, "Ma man's got a heart like a rock cast in the sea." He later explained that his aim was "to combine ragtime syncopation with a real melody in the spiritual tradition."

In her autobiography, Ethel says she made her start in vaudeville on her birthday in 1917 (page 71) and shortly after teamed with the Hill Sisters (page 76). She talks later (page 94) about the Mills Sisters (including Florence) and the Hill Sisters being confused with one another, and she refers to the trio having Kinky (Ethel Caldwell) as one of the "sisters." However, according to Florence Mills's biographer, Bill Egan, "I have the *Chicago Defender* for May 22, 1915 showing the 'Three Hill Sisters' (hence including Ethel Waters as well as the original two) playing the Dixie Theatre in DC and Mills and Kinky (Florence and Ethel Caldwell) playing the Palace Theater DC in the same week. Then on June 26, 1915 the *Defender* has Mills and Kinky at the S H Dudley Theater in DC and the Three Hills Sisters at the Lincoln Theatre Pittsburgh."[1] So the date of Ethel's professional career predates the year 1917 given in her autobiography.

At first, Sweet Mama Stringbean toured the Carnival, or "Kerosene Circuit," with the Hill Sisters. Then, for several years, she earned a living by touring black vaudeville houses in the South. Ethel signed with Theatre Owners Booking Association (TOBA), which booked acts for the small-time Southern black vaudeville circuit. Champ Clark describes this organization as

> a prime avenue for African American entertainers attempting to make a life in show business, or a life anywhere for that matter. Organised in 1909, the TOBA, its acronym known among performers to stand for "Tough On Black Asses," came to represent nearly 100 theatres throughout the South and Southeast. Also known as "Toby Time" and the "chitlin' circuit," life on the TOBA was hard and tough, its black performers traveling through Jim Crow [racially segregated] states where lynching was common, separate and unequal was the law, and shows, as Ethel Waters recalled, "ran from 9 in the AM until unconscious." Still, the TOBA provided a stage to many of the great African American entertainers who rose to prominence in the early through mid-20th Century.[2]

Some theatres in the South were owned or managed by dangerous racists who, while making money from black performers and audiences, displayed open hostility toward them. In the early 1920s Ethel was engaged to appear in Atlanta with her partner (and lover), dancer Ethel Williams (see chapter 3), and accompanist Pearl Wright. Says Mel Watkins:

> Charles P. Bailey, owner of Atlanta's 81 Decatur Street Theatre, was one of many. Described by Ethel Waters as a "tough-bitten old Georgia cracker," Bailey was one of the most powerful men in Atlanta during the teens and twenties and, with the help of local police, ran his theatre like an antebellum plantation. According to Waters, he often harassed female performers; after an argument, he beat Bessie Smith and had her thrown in jail. During a heated

disagreement about working conditions, Waters responded to one of Bailey's outbursts ("No Yankee nigger bitch is telling me how to run my theatre") with, "You and no other cracker sonofabitch can tell me what to do." Leaving her fee and many of her costumes behind, Waters had to sneak as far enough out of town by horse and buggy to get to an out-of-the-way railroad station where she could buy a ticket to leave Atlanta and escape Bailey's fury.[3]

The two Ethels and Pearl managed to escape from Atlanta and travel to Nashville, where Ethel planned to lodge a complaint about Bailey to the head of the TOBA. However, before making the complaint, she couldn't resist visiting a Western Union office and sending a telegram to the "Georgia cracker" that read, "Who got effed this time?"

Ethel first arrived in New York around 1919, and she quickly became a popular attraction in Harlem nightclubs such as Edmond's Cellar, a basement dive or speakeasy at 132nd Street and Fifth Avenue. She described this as "the last stop on the way down in show business" but remained there until 1923, with occasional breaks for appearances in vaudeville. Ethel's engagement at Edmond's resulted in an offer to make her first recordings. The blues recording boom started in 1920, when Mamie Smith's recording of "Crazy Blues" sold 75,000 copies within the first month of its release and more than half a million within the next half year in the black community. Consequently, the music industry discovered a whole new market for "race records" by black artists for black record buyers. The success of race records created a search for black talent, and Ethel soon found herself in a recording studio. On March 21, 1921, when Ethel made her first recordings—"The New York Glide"/"At the New Jump Steady Ball" for Cardinal Records in New York—she became the fourth black woman to record in the 1920s. Her predecessors were Mamie Smith (February 1920), Lucille Hegamin (December 1920), and Mary Stafford (January 1921). Almost immediately she was signed by Black Swan Records in New York, one of the few black-owned record companies. Owners W. C. Handy and Harry H. Pace signed Ethel, and she recorded more than twenty songs, including the best-selling "Down Home Blues," "Jazzin' Babies Blues," "Memphis Man," and "All the Time." While making records for Black Swan, between 1921 and 1923, Pace sent Ethel out on tour with the Black Swan Troubadours, a band led by Fletcher Henderson.

In 1922, Ethel received top billing in a touring revue called *Oh Joy!* Her lover, Ethel Williams, was also in the cast. It was in this show that Ethel devised a show-stopping introduction to her song "Georgia Blues":

Noting that Ma Rainey had often made her entrance onto the stage by stepping out of a mock-up of a Victrola record machine, Waters came up with what she considered a classier opening. It consisted of remaining in the back of the theatre, out of the audience's view, while another artist, in this case the dancer Ethel Williams, entered onto the stage and called out to her partner in vain: "Where's that Ethel Waters? What can be keeping her? How can I start that act without that gal?" Peering out into the darkness, looking toward the back of the room, Williams would then call out, "Are you Ethel Waters?" That was Waters's cue to make a grand, blustering entrance down the aisle, and as she approached the stage, she would yell, "I ain't Bessie Smith!" Then, she would step onto the stage dressed in a plain, gingham dress, wearing a straw hat, as if she were a simple girl from the South, and sing "Georgia Blues."[4]

Ethel had left the cast of *Oh Joy!* before it opened on Broadway, thus making *Africana* (1927) her Broadway debut. In 1923 she engaged Pearl Wright as her pianist, and she appears on most of Ethel's recordings until 1929. Ethel couldn't read music, so Pearl, a former school teacher who could read music, helped her out.

For several years, Ethel toured in vaudeville with Earl Dancer, who, though he was not married to her, was sometimes described as her "husband." An item in *Billboard* (August 16, 1924) notes: "Perhaps the high spot of the season is the spectacular rise into prominence of Ethel Waters, the first colored woman in years to command a route and stellar salary on the Keith or Orpheum time. She, with her husband Earl Dancer, has contracts for forty weeks that bear high figures." Throughout the 1920s, Earl Dancer would prove to be an important influence on Ethel.

In 1925, Ethel replaced Florence Mills at the smart Plantation Club, situated above the Winter Garden Theatre on Broadway at 50th Street in midManhattan. Florence was one of the most popular black stars of the 1920s. In Britain she was described by show business impresario C. B. Cochran as "one of the greatest artists who ever walked on to a stage," but her career was cut short by her untimely death at the age of thirty-one in 1927. Earl Dancer persuaded Ethel to audition. According to Florence's biographer, Bill Egan, "Ethel believed 'Broadway and all downtown belonged to Florence Mills.' At the audition, however, Ethel not only got the job but also a new song to introduce. 'Dinah' proved to be a big success for her."[5] Ethel's engagement at the Plantation Club marked a turning point in her career, for "Dinah" became the first international hit to emerge from a nightclub revue. Ethel had already signed a ten-year contract with another recording company, Columbia Records, and she made her first recordings for that label in April 1925. She immortalized "Dinah" on record on October 20 that year, and it became one of her biggest-selling records.

Bill Egan adds that, from the chorus, Josephine Baker seized the opportunity to become Ethel's stand-in when Ethel was ill. She had learned all of Ethel's songs and was ready for such an opportunity. Josephine was sensational, and luckily her performance was seen by Caroline Reagan, an American-born Paris resident. Josephine later recalls a confrontation with Ethel in her autobiography: "The next evening I found violets in the dressing room and Ethel on the stage. I couldn't believe my eyes. She had been ordered to bed for two weeks. . . . It was back to the chorus again. When I ran into Ethel in the wings she gave me a furious look. That was the last straw. 'Back so soon? Too bad for the show,' I snapped. Ethel was so startled by my rudeness that she muttered something like 'stupid darky.' I'm sure she would have pulled my hair if it hadn't been so short. I was ashamed of us both."[6] For Josephine, the payoff came when Caroline Reagan had the idea of staging a black revue in Paris, to be called *La Revue Negre*: "Her first preference was Florence. . . . Ethel Waters, still wary of overseas performing, deliberately demanded an excessive amount. Josephine's performance had impressed Caroline Reagan, who offered her the lead in *La Revue Negre*."[7] Josephine sailed for Paris on September 15, 1925—and *La Revue Negre* established her in France, where she became a legend.

Ten years later, at the height of her popularity in Europe, a triumphant Josephine returned to New York to star on Broadway in *Ziegfeld Follies*. At the same time, Ethel was the toast of Broadway in *At Home Abroad* (see chapter 5). Two black stars in white shows on Broadway. Comparisons were inevitable. However, for Josephine, the comparison between herself and the star she had once understudied at the Plantation Club was a sore subject. Josephine was not kind to Ethel, and she is quoted on the subject by one of her biographers, Phyllis Rose: "Any artist must develop a technique of his own, and I have tried to avoid singing 'colored mammy, back to Alabammy' songs. Not all Negroes have to jump around as though they were monkeys or African savages. Besides, I sing soprano, and that would hardly adapt itself to the traditional blues and other Beale Street ballads." Rose adds, "What she meant by her snide remarks about Ethel Waters was that she was glad she hadn't had to make a career of being black."[8] It was unfair of Josephine to describe Ethel's songs as "colored mammy, back to Alabammy" material. Irving Berlin's "Supper Time," about a lynching in the south, which Ethel had performed in the revue *As Thousands Cheer* (1933), could hardly be described in that way. It is more likely that Ethel's clever and funny send-up of Josephine in the same revue, singing Berlin's "Harlem on My Mind," is what upset the expatriate. It is reported that during her run in *Follies*, Josephine refused to receive Ethel, who had called to pay her "professional respects."[9] As it turned out, *At Home Abroad* was Ethel's second Broadway success in a "white" show (see chapter 5), while Josephine's *Follies* was a disaster. She subsequently returned to Paris.

Ten years after her confrontation with Josephine, history repeated itself when Ethel upset another rising black star, Billie Holiday. In February 1935, the teenager was sent to Philadelphia for an audition at the Lincoln Theatre. Ethel was on the bill, and Billie was looking forward to taking part in the show. She later recalls in her autobiography, coauthored with William Dufty:

> I still remember that shaky moment I got up on the stage to audition. I told the piano player to give me "Underneath the Harlem Moon," which was real popular then. I hadn't finished the first chorus when Ethel Waters bounced up in the darkened theatre. "Nobody's going to sing on this goddam stage," she boomed, "but Ethel Waters and the Brown Sisters." That settled that. "Underneath the Harlem Moon" was Miss Waters' big number. But nobody told me. . . . So the stage manager handed me two dollars and told me to get on the bus and go home. I threw the money at him and told him to kiss my ass and tell Miss Waters to do the same. . . . Later on Miss Waters was quoted as saying that I sang like "my shoes were too tight." I don't know why Ethel Waters didn't like me. I never did a thing to her that I know of except sing her big number that day for my big Philly audition.[10]

In 1974 music critic Henry Pleasants published *The Great American Popular Singers*, one of the earliest and most perceptive books on the art of jazz and popular singing. In his chapter about Billie, he compares her to Ethel and offers some interesting insights into their backgrounds and singing styles:

> Many elements in the Billie Holiday story recall the career of Ethel Waters. Both were children of the Northern slums. Both were born illegitimately to slum children, and both were grownups before they were even properly adolescent. . . . Both did menial work, Ethel as a scullery and chambermaid, Billie scrubbing the famous white steps of Baltimore's brick row houses. Both served a rough, tough apprenticeship as singers. . . . Ethel was the stronger character of the two, certainly the more self-reliant. Billie fought, and fought hard, both against society and against the person that society had made of her. . . . Her career and Ethel Waters', after Harlem, differed considerably and significantly. Their respective ages had something to do with it. Ethel, twenty years older than Billie, was early enough on the scene to make a career in both black and white vaudeville, a preparation that revealed the talent and established the professional accomplishments for her subsequent triumphs as an actress. . . . Ethel was, in any case, far more a woman of the theatre than Lady Day, not only in terms of experience, but also in terms of disposition and predilection,

and it showed in her singing. In just about every song that Ethel Waters ever sang she projected a character. Hers was, indeed, an art of characterisation, whether she was playing a part or singing a song. Billie Holiday never projected anybody but Billie.[11]

It is a myth that Ethel was hostile to all other black female singers. Tensions clearly surfaced with Josephine and Billie, but throughout their lives they displayed just as many fits of temperament as Ethel. Singer Adelaide Hall was anything but temperamental. Born in Brooklyn, New York, Ethel first encountered "sweet" Adelaide, who was still in her teens, at Edmond's Cellar when the youngster was starting out on her singing career. It was an eventful journey that took her to acclaim in Paris and London and lasted into the 1990s. Iain Cameron Williams describes Ethel's generosity toward Adelaide at Edmond's Cellar in *Underneath a Harlem Moon: The Harlem to Paris Years of Adelaide Hall*:

> Ethel became accustomed to seeing Adelaide around the place and offered to help her develop her act. Adelaide's talent and genuine enthusiasm made her an easy pupil to coach. She paid careful attention as Ethel worked the room. Her technique and delivery seemed effortless and her clever use of sexual innuendoes had the audience eating out of the palm of her hand. Adelaide soon realised that if she could project herself confidently in front of a half-baked audience, she could easily win the admiration of a sober crowd. Ethel taught her the art of voice control.[12]

In 1934 Adelaide succeeded Ethel as the star attraction of the Cotton Club (see chapter 4), and though Adelaide made London her home in 1939, they remained friends. Adelaide always spoke highly of her. In her later years, Adelaide found she had something in common with Ethel. In spite of being the true first ladies of jazz (not Billie or Ella Fitzgerald), their pioneering work in the field has been undervalued by most critics and historians. After the death of Florence Mills, it was Adelaide who inherited her crown as the most celebrated black female star in America when she starred on Broadway in the hit revue *Blackbirds of 1928*. Josephine Baker was mainly famous in her adopted home of France, and Ethel did not become a major star until the 1930s. As singers, Ethel and Adelaide were the trailblazers who paved the way for the likes of Billie and Ella; unfortunately it has been a secret no one has cared to make public.[13]

Throughout the 1920s, Ethel persistently refused to perform in white vaudeville houses—what African Americans called "the white time"—because she feared that white audiences wouldn't understand her work. However, Earl

Dancer convinced her to try. After auditioning in Chicago, Ethel found herself on the Keith circuit—known as the white big time. Consequently, Ethel became one of the first black entertainers to move successfully from black vaudeville and nightclubs to "the white time." Caribbean-born comedian Bert Williams had done this earlier in the *Ziegfeld Follies*, but he was allowed to perform on stage only in blackface. Donald Bogle comments:

> Gradually, during this time, Waters' work took on a new sophistication, and her stage presence cooled down some to the point where this mix of ghetto raunch and rowdiness, this exotique, had become, in the words of Alberta Hunter, "a very refined performer." Her big twenties hits "Dinah" and "Sweet Georgia Brown" were smooth, easygoing pop tunes. More than any other star of the period, she legitmized the Harlem clubs. Whites were going uptown to see this woman who could sing songs by important white composers in a new *cullid* way.[14]

Ethel made her debut in Broadway musical theatre in a revue called *Africana*. Opening at Daly's 63rd Street Theatre on July 11, 1927, it was produced by Earl Dancer, who is often credited as having "discovered" Ethel. After leaving the Plantation Club in September 1925, she had toured with Dancer in a "tab" show called *Miss Calico*. *Miss Calico* and various other tab shows featuring Ethel were patched together for *Africana*. Other African Americans who contributed to the show include Donald Heyward, who wrote the music and lyrics, and Louis Douglas, who staged the dances. In the middle of the second act, Ethel stopped the show with a medley of her hit songs including "Dinah," "Shake That Thing," "Take Your Black Bottom Outside," and "I'm Coming Virginia." The New York critics raved about her, and three years later, James Weldon Johnson, one of the leading lights of the Harlem Renaissance, enthused: "It was a swift modern revue. There were several quite clever people in it, but Ethel Waters dominated the show. She did this nearly to the same degree that Florence Mills dominated her show, but with a technique almost in contrast. Miss Waters is tall, almost statuesque, with a head so beautiful that Antonio Salemme asked the privilege of doing it in bronze— the piece was purchased by Carl Van Vechten. . . . Miss Waters gets her audiences, and she does get them completely, through an innate poise that she possesses; through the quiet and subtlety of her personality."[15]

Ethel's second Broadway show, *Lew Leslie's Blackbirds* (also known as *Blackbirds of 1930*) opened at the Royale Theatre on October 22, 1930. Florence Mills, Adelaide Hall, and Bill "Bojangles" Robinson had all starred in previous editions of Lew Leslie's popular *Blackbirds* revues. In addition to Ethel, for the 1930 edition, he also hired Flournoy Miller, the Berry Brothers, and Buck and Bubbles. Though it resembled its predecessors of the 1920s, this version was not warmly received by the critics. However, they did praise Ethel and song-writers Eubie Blake (who also conducted the orchestra) and Andy Razaf. Blake wrote "You're Lucky to Me" for Ethel, and this takeoff on the popular white crooner Rudy Vallee was one of her best numbers in the show. Ethel comments in her autobiography: "*Blackbirds* opened . . . at a theatre right next to a flea circus. Our show was a flop and the fleas outdrew us at every performance."[16]

It was during the run of *Blackbirds* that Mary Lou Williams substituted for Pearl Wright as Ethel's accompanist. Mary, who went on to become one of the most celebrated jazz pianists of her time, is quoted by her biographer, Linda Dahl:

> "Pearl had to go away and sat with me for at least a week teaching me how to accompany Ethel Waters because I'd have to play for her while she was absent." Evidently it went very well. Five years later (in December 1936), Ethel Waters pleaded with Mary by telegram to drop everything and come with her on tour. "What a beautiful, tall woman, and so kind," Mary wrote of that complex personality. "I used to hear how Ethel would take her big car and chauffeur to a very poor Negro section, fill her car with poor kids and take them downtown to buy them clothing."[17]

After *Blackbirds*, Lew Leslie tried again with *Rhapsody in Black*, also starring Ethel, which opened at the Sam H. Harris Theatre on May 4, 1931. Allen Woll comments:

> Though Waters had been popular in the *Blackbirds* revue, Leslie moved to eliminate her from *Rhapsody in Black* because of her high salary. While Waters was on a vaudeville tour, Leslie built the show around a talented newcomer, Valaida (Snow), who not only played the trumpet but also conducted the orchestra in one number. Waters, who was under contract for Leslie's new production, suddenly found herself without anything to do, and she complained bitterly . . . she turned the matter over to her lawyer. He reminded Leslie of a clause that stated that Waters had to be satisfied with her material for the show, so they searched for the appropriate songwriter.[18]

A newly discovered husband-and-wife team, Mann Holiner and Alberta Nichols, provided Ethel with some of the biggest hits in the show, including "Washtub Rhapsody (Rub-sody)" and the lovely "You Can't Stop Me from Loving You," which Ethel recorded on June 16, 1931. Allen Woll describes how this new material altered her stage persona forever:

> Not only were these songs successful . . . they also revealed a new side to the Waters persona. Everyone was expecting the traditional off-color numbers, but

these songs emphasized her acting ability. She created new and believable characters for each sequence. Leslie, of course, later took credit for this change. . . . Leslie told Waters that "I'm going to have you sing character songs, and give character portraits of your people. No more 'hot' numbers for you." Ethel Waters was stunned. "But you can't do that, Mr. Leslie," she protested. "I've always got by with scorching lyrics." Leslie, however, was adamant and as much as Miss Waters dreaded losing her identity by venturing into a new field, she accepted the assignment and in *Rhapsody in Black* emerged a new and far superior actress. . . . Waters' triumph catapulted her into Broadway's top-drawing and highest-paid elite.[19]

Meanwhile, in *La Sirene des Tropiques* (1927), produced in France, Josephine Baker became the first black actress to star in an international feature film. However, Ethel was the first black star to be prominently featured in a Hollywood movie. At the beginning of the sound era, in the rush to produce musicals, Hollywood eagerly signed all types of singers. In *On with the Show!* Ethel didn't have a starring role, but she made an impact all the same. Produced by Warner Bros. and released in May 1929, the film was advertised as "the first all-colour, all-talking, all-singing" film. Featuring many top artistes of the time, including Joe E. Brown and Betty Compson, it is a backstage-onstage musical, and the entire action takes place during an evening's performance of a Broadway musical during its out-of-town tryout. Almost without exception, Ethel's guest appearance was considered the musical highlight. A reviewer in the British journal *The Melody Maker* offers the following: "There is nothing of particular interest to musicians other than the singing of Ethel Waters, who gives an excellent hot rendering of 'Birmingham Bertha' and 'Am I Blue?' Miss Waters has a very strong personality, and although she can be heard singing these songs on H.M.V. records, it is undoubtedly worth while going to see her 'in person' on the screen."[20] It is worth noting that the lyrics for Ethel's two songs were written by one of the best lyricists of his generation: Grant Clarke. He had earlier written special material for Bert Williams, Fanny Brice, and Al Jolson. His other compositions include "Second Hand Rose," popularized by Fanny Brice, and "I'm a Little Blackbird Looking for a Bluebird," made famous by Florence Mills. It was the composer of these songs, Harry Akst, who was responsible for bringing Ethel to the attention of the producer of the film, Darryl F. Zanuck. Ethel held her own with the tough movie mogul Zanuck and was paid handsomely for her guest appearance in his movie. Says Donald Bogle:

> Waters became the first African American woman to deal with Hollywood on her *own* terms. Perhaps what bolstered Waters's confidence was the simple fact that she didn't take Hollywood very seriously. She thought of herself as a New

York club and recording star, and though she hadn't yet triumphed on Broadway, she had hopes of doing so. She didn't need movies. With only two numbers to perform in *On With the Show!*, Waters knew her performances were considered by the studio to be a *specialty act*, which soon became the way most studios usually handled big-name Negro performers. Rather than cast the black stars as characters integral to the film's story line, they simply filmed their musical numbers. . . . The studio offered Waters an extra thousand dollars if she'd dub the voice of white star Betty Compson singing. But Waters refused: no way was her voice going to be heard coming out of someone else's body. Completing her work, Ethel Waters packed her bags, got out of town, and resumed her tour on the Orpheum circuit. But in subsequent years, Hollywood would bring her back.[21]

In *A Song in the Dark: The Birth of the Musical Film*, Richard Barrios gives a detailed analysis of *On with the Show!* and praises Ethel's participation:

Best of all, there's a treasurable contribution by one of the greatest American singers. Ethel Waters has only the briefest opportunity to interact with the white performers on or off stage, and given a greater chance she would have stolen the film even more than she does with her two songs. With a persona far removed from her later incarnation of revival-meeting earth-grandmother, she's slim and cheeky, the same Waters who earned early fame as "Sweet Mama Stringbean." For "Am I Blue?" she's done up as a peculiarly chic cotton-picker, belting torchy and hot. After an absence of an hour, she returns in high style for "Birmingham Bertha." Cotton field and headrag have been swapped for an urban street and flapper feathers as Waters invades Chicago to reclaim her man. Snarling and purring, mugging her way through Clarke's lyrics, she projects more musical authority than anyone since Jolson. The briefness of her appearance is as regrettable as the fact that her film work was so sparse. In general, *On With the Show!* is an engaging and significant antique; Ethel Waters's participation ensures that for just a moment it becomes the celebration of one person's art.[22]

In 2004 professor Edward Mapp screened one of Ethel's sequences from *On with the Show!* during a lecture on black cinema at Indiana University. He showed video footage to illustrate the development of African Americans in films, including Ethel singing "Am I Blue?" He says: "I was surprised because at this particular lecture some Professors came over and said, 'Thank God you didn't bring Bessie Smith. We're so used to seeing her in that short film *St. Louis Blues*.' They loved seeing Ethel in that clip. They were enthusiastic because they hadn't seen it before. And it was a long sequence in which some white extras can be seen off-stage watching her in awe from the wings. And you realise this was a woman who could really capture an audience. It was magnificent."[23]

Ethel could have had her first starring role in MGM's *Hallelujah!*, which was released on August 20, 1929. She was the first choice of the film's director, King Vidor, but lost the part to a sixteen-year-old chorus girl named Nina Mae McKinney when "the talent man King Vidor sent East to wave gold bags at me was stalled on the job by colored theatrical people unfriendly to me."[24] Consequently it was Nina, not Ethel, who was given the chance to be the first black actress to play a leading role in a Hollywood film. Later that year, in addition to Ethel and Nina, two other black women made an impact in films, but these appearances were made outside Hollywood in short films produced at the Astoria Studios in Long Island, New York. They were Bessie Smith in *St. Louis Blues*, released on September 8, and Fredi Washington (opposite Duke Ellington) in *Black and Tan Fantasy*, released on October 29. The only other leading film roles played by black women at this time were in movies produced independently, outside Hollywood, by filmmakers such as African American Oscar Micheaux.

Even if Ethel had played the lead in *Hallelujah!* she would have faced discrimination in Hollywood. MGM signed Nina Mae McKinney to a five-year contract on the strength of her success in the film, but she was the first of many black leading ladies to discover there were no follow-up roles. In the 1930s Hollywood wasn't ready to promote a black star, and the only roles available were simpleminded maids. Four years passed before Ethel appeared on film again.

In 1933 Ethel costarred with seven-year-old Sammy Davis Jr. in Vitaphone's *Rufus Jones for President*. This was a twenty-minute short musical comedy, directed by Roy Mack and filmed in the Warner Bros. studio in Brooklyn, New York. Sammy played Rufus Jones, who dreams he is elected president of the United States. Ethel was cast as Rufus's "mammy," who is elected his vice president. Her songs included "Am I Blue?" and "Underneath a Harlem Moon." It might have been a charming fantasy, but despite Ethel's wonderful singing and young Sammy's spectacular singing and dancing, the film is full of derogatory and offensive racial stereotypes involving chickens, watermelons, and crapshooting. Henry T. Sampson states that "brilliant performances by Ethel Waters and Sammy Davis, Jr. are marred by scenes showing blacks, in roles as U. S. Senators, checking razors, shooting craps in the halls of Congress, and passing laws to make chicken—and watermelon—stealing legal. From a historical view, however, black musicals made during this period are the only existing record on film of black music and dance performed by many of the best American entertainers of the era."[25]

Ethel also starred in *Bubbling Over* (1934), another short (twenty-minute) musical that was full of stereotypes but redeemed by Ethel's singing. The story centers on a group of Harlem folks who sit around waiting for dinner. Ethel has a thankless role as the wife of a lazy, good-for-nothing janitor; she reacts to her shiftless husband's malingering with anger and despair. Only an artiste as great as Ethel had the talent to turn one of her numbers, "Darkies Never Dream," into a moving comment on broken dreams and lost hopes. According to Mel Watkins, "Her curiously blasé version of the mournful 'Darkies Never Dream'—delivered over a washboard with a bandana tied about her head—is as ironic as it is poignant."[26]

Ethel's film career did not take off in a big way until Hollywood beckoned in 1942 (see chapter 6). Meanwhile, there was one further guest appearance in a Hollywood production, Universal's *Gift of Gab* (1934), in which she sang "I Ain't Gonna Sin No More." In addition to Ethel, the guest stars included Ruth Etting, Boris Karloff, and Bela Lugosi, but the film was a flop. In *The Hollywood Musical*, Clive Hirschhorn describes this movie as "shapeless and cumbersome. . . . Over thirty big name performers tried to salvage it with their respective skills but to no avail, proving, once and for all, that if you're saddled with a stinker, you're saddled with a stinker."[27]

Notes

1. Bill Egan, by e-mail, August 2, 2006.

2. Champ Clark, *Shuffling to Ignominy: The Tragedy of Stepin Fetchit* (Lincoln: iUniverse, 2005), 12.

3. Mel Watkins, *On the Real Side: A History of African American Comedy from Slavery to Chris Rock* (New York: Simon and Schuster, 1999), 366–67.

4. Randall Cherry, "Ethel Waters: Long, Lean, Lanky Mama," in Robert Springer, ed., *Nobody Knows Where the Blues Come From: Lyrics and History* (Jackson: University Press of Mississippi, 2005), 268.

5. Bill Egan, *Florence Mills: Harlem Jazz Queen* (Lanham, Md.: Scarecrow Press, 2004), 135.

6. Josephine Baker and Jo Bouillon, trans. Mariana Fitzpatrick, *Josephine* (New York: Harper and Row, 1977), 40–41.

7. Egan, *Florence Mills*, 135.

8. Phyllis Rose, *Jazz Cleopatra: Josephine Baker in Her Time* (New York: Doubleday, 1989), 170.

9. Jean-Claude Baker and Chris Chase, *Josephine: The Hungry Heart* (Holbrook, Mass.: Adams, 1993), 198.

10. Billie Holiday and William Dufty, *Lady Sings the Blues* (New York: Doubleday, 1956), 63–64.

11. Henry Pleasants, *The Great American Popular Singers* (London: Gollancz, 1974), 160–62.

12. Iain Cameron Williams, *Underneath a Harlem Moon: The Harlem to Paris Years of Adelaide Hall* (London: Continuum, 2002), 55.

13. Stephen Bourne, "The Real First Lady of Jazz," *The Guardian*, January 25, 2003, 16.

14. Donald Bogle, *Brown Sugar: Eighty Years of America's Black Female Superstars* (New York: Harmony, 1980), 52.

15. James Weldon Johnson, *Black Manhattan* (New York: Knopf, 1930), 209–10.

16. Ethel Waters with Charles Samuels, *His Eye Is on the Sparrow* (New York: Da Capo, 1992), 214.

17. Linda Dahl, *Morning Glory: A Biography of Mary Lou Williams* (Berkeley: University of California Press, 1999), 82.

18. Allen Woll, *Black Musical Theatre: From Coontown to Dreamgirls* (Baton Rouge: Louisiana State University Press, 1989), 147.

19. Woll, *Black Musical Theatre*, 147–48.

20. Unidentified reviewer, *The Melody Maker*, December 1929, 11.

21. Donald Bogle, *Bright Boulevards, Bold Dreams: The Story of Black Hollywood* (New York: One World, 2005), 85–86.

22. Richard Barrios, *A Song in the Dark: The Birth of the Musical Film* (New York: Oxford University Press, 1995), 103.

23. Edward Mapp, interview with Stephen Bourne, London, August 15, 2005.

24. Waters, *Sparrow*, 198.

25. Henry T. Sampson, *Blacks in Black and White: A Source Book on Black Films*, 2nd ed. (Metuchen, N.J.: Scarecrow Press, 1995), 232.

26. Watkins, *On the Real Side*, 196.

27. Clive Hirschhorn, *The Hollywood Musical* (London: Octopus, 1981), 92.

CHAPTER THREE

~

Paris, London, and Being in the Life

Very little documentation exists of Ethel's trip to Paris in 1929, other than the reminiscences she shares in her 1951 autobiography. She mentions some friends she encountered, including the Berry Brothers, who were cast members of the successful Broadway revue *Blackbirds*. This show enjoyed a long run in New York before transferring to the Moulin Rouge, with singer Adelaide Hall taking the lead. Also in the cast was Elisabeth Welch, who loved Paris and, like many other African American visitors, discovered the atmosphere more relaxed, compared with America. It was in Paris that Elisabeth met Ethel:

> She was adorable, a lovely charming person. Gentle, quiet and nice. She was a marvellous singer, had a lovely face and she had fun. She didn't like everybody, especially girl singers. After I met her she gave Billie Holiday and Lena Horne a hard time, but fortunately she liked me, even though I was a singer. But unlike Billie and Lena, I wasn't a rival, and I didn't threaten her position. I found her an ordinary person, not educated, and somewhat shy. I think she wanted to be friendly but didn't know how. I saw her again in New York after the war. It must have been about 1946. She was at a very low point in her career. In her younger days Ethel Waters was thin and quite attractive. She only got heavy later on when she became religious and her eye was on the sparrow![1]

Ethel also encountered Bricktop, an African American entertainer who became the most famous nightclub owner in prewar Paris (1926–1939). Her nightclub attracted all the famous society people of the day. Among

21

her distinguished guests, who often performed unannounced, were Noel Coward, Duke Ellington, the Prince of Wales, and Paul Robeson. Bricktop and Josephine Baker became friends during this time. One of her other friends, Cole Porter, wrote "Miss Otis Regrets" for her (this was recorded by Ethel in 1934). In her autobiography, Bricktop remembers Ethel's trip to Paris: "She was the talk of the town, but she took me aside and confided, 'Brick, I'm starving to death.' It wasn't a matter of money, but of food. Right in the middle of Paris, with all those fabulous restaurants, Ethel was starving for some real American food, so I let her move into my place for about three weeks and she cooked greens to her heart's content. Ethel was never one to stay out or to drink. I was able to turn Paris for her from a nightmare into a place where she could really enjoy herself in her own way."[2]

If Bricktop was the expatriate who welcomed black visitors to Paris in the 1920s and 1930s, then in London it was John Payne, an African American baritone and choirmaster who remained in London after visiting in 1919 with the Southern Syncopated Orchestra. It was through his friendship with a liberal-minded aristocrat, Lady Mary Cook, that Payne had been able to acquire a home at 17 Regents Park Road. The back of the house was opposite the famous zoo in the beautifully manicured Regents Park. This was bordered on the near side by a row of some of London's most aristocratic homes. Payne's home became a focal point for expatriate or visiting African Americans, especially from the world of music, and these included Ethel.

Lady Cook was the daughter of Viscount Bridgeport, the half brother of Viscount Nelson, England's greatest naval hero, and she was the wife of Sir Herbert Cook, a wealthy businessman as well as an art critic and collector. He was a trustee of the National Gallery and had one of the largest private art collections in England. Among the six hundred paintings in his house were two works by Rembrandt. Lady Cook happily subsidized Payne's hospitality, and she had a special, if paternalistic, attraction to black people, whom she insisted should call her Mother. There was no sexual relationship between Cook and Payne because he was homosexual. He cared very much for Lady Cook and benefited from the lifestyle she provided.

For African American musicians and singers who visited Europe, Payne had the reputation of being their ambassador, and most of them found their way to his home, if not for a place to stay, at least for introductions to new friends in the entertainment and social circles of England. In addition to Ethel, Adelaide Hall stayed there with her husband in 1931 when she accepted an offer to headline at the London Palladium. Contralto Marian Anderson lived at Payne's house following her arrival in London in November

1927, and she recalls this first trip to Europe in her autobiography: "Life in London for me centred largely around the house in Regents Park Road. I spent most of my time in it when I was not out taking lessons. I should add that I did some voice work with Amanda Ira Aldridge, daughter of Ira Aldridge, the famous actor."[3] In 1928 blues singer Alberta Hunter stayed with Payne when she accepted an offer to play Queenie, opposite Paul Robeson's Joe, in the London version of *Show Boat*. When Paul Robeson stayed with Payne on his first visit to London in 1922, he befriended another guest, Lawrence Brown, a gentle, charming man who had come to Europe to accompany Roland Hayes, the concert singer who gave a command performance for King George V. According to Robeson's biographer, Martin Bauml Duberman, "One night at the Payne's, Robeson sang a few songs 'just for fun,' and thirty years later Larry Brown recalled that he 'knew at once that it was possible for him to become a great singer.' Remembering Robeson's marvellous voice, he later sent him the published volume of spirituals; ultimately he would become Robeson's musical collaborator and friend."[4]

After Robeson made London his home in 1928, John Payne continued to play a role in his life. He was hired as the chorus master of *Show Boat* at the Theatre Royal, Drury Lane, and this was the production in which Robeson sang "Old Man River" for the first time. Robeson often attended and sometimes sang at the open-house parties Payne gave on Sundays in his Regents Park Road drawing room. Payne also worked as an "extra" in some of Robeson's British films, including *King Solomon's Mines* (1937). At the outbreak of the Second World War in 1939, Payne and Lady Cook moved away from London to a new home in Cornwall. She died in 1943, and Payne passed away in 1952.

Unlike her trip to Paris, Ethel's visit to London has been thoroughly researched and documented by jazz historian Howard Rye. In a 1986 edition of the jazz and blues journal *Storyville*,[5] Rye includes a useful "British Diary" for Ethel, which reveals that she made her London debut at the Palladium on November 25, 1929, billed as "the ebony comedienne star of the talkie *On With the Show!*" Her repertoire included "Georgia Blues," "Go Back Where You Stayed Last Night," and "Am I Blue?" Other appearances included the Café de Paris and the Holborn Empire. On February 11, 1930, Ethel broadcast for the British Broadcasting Corporation (BBC) in a radio program called *Vaudeville*. She is billed in the *Radio Times* as "The Famous American Star," and others featured in the lineup included popular comedian Wee Georgie Wood and Jack Payne and his BBC Dance Orchestra.

Ethel made many friends in Paris and London, including a member of the royal family. In her autobiography, Ethel recalls meeting the Prince of Wales at the Café de Paris. In 1936, before he was crowned as King Edward VIII, he abdicated in favor of his brother, George VI. Thereafter he was known as the Duke of Windsor. The prince had a soft spot for African American music, and he particularly enjoyed listening to black women singers. He had been a big fan of Florence Mills, star of the popular London edition of the *Blackbirds* revue. One evening Ethel arrived at the Café de Paris to find the prince sitting at her table with a lady friend: "He was incognito, and when he was told he was at my table he came over and apologized. I told His Royal Highness that it was okay. I didn't like it later when he abdicated. . . . After all, he was the only king who had ever apologized to me for anything. The Prince came back once a week to catch my act during the ten weeks I played at the Café de Paris [December 1929 to February 1930]. He always nodded to me and I always nodded back."[6] Ethel returned home to New York City on March 12, 1930, on the Cunard liner *Aquitania.*

John Payne was a homosexual, but this was not public knowledge during his lifetime. In fact, the sexuality of many African Americans who were in the public eye in the 1920s and 1930s was kept private, and these included Ethel, who in the early 1920s lived in Harlem with her girlfriend, Ethel Williams. Lesbian and gay nightlife thrived during the Harlem Renaissance in New York's Greenwich Village and Harlem, and in addition to Langston Hughes, there were a number of black gay literary figures associated with the renaissance. These include Claude McKay, Countee Cullen, and Alain Locke. Wealthy white gay writer and photographer Carl Van Vechten became a patron of the Harlem Renaissance and befriended and promoted many of its major figures, including Hughes, Richard Wright, Bessie Smith, and Ethel, who commented that Van Vechten knew more about Harlem than any other white man except the captain of the Harlem police station! Van Vechten believed that Ethel and Langston Hughes "had more genius than any others of their race in this country."[7]

Ethel's lesbianism has been conspicuous by its absence in the many books that have documented her life and career, notably her own autobiographies. With the exception of Tina Gianoulis's entry in *The Queer Encyclopedia of Film and Television* (2005), Ethel isn't mentioned in any books written about lesbian and gay history, but this may have something to do with the fact that so few people knew about Ethel's sexuality. Perhaps the most revealing insights into Ethel's "secret life" have come from interviews with expatriate Elisabeth Welch, who introduced "Stormy Weather" to British audiences in 1933, and Mabel Hampton (1902–1989), a former domestic worker and dancer. Elisabeth said she knew Ethel's name when she was a kid "because she was a big name and a great artist. In the 1920s she lived in the bad part of Harlem, a rather poor area. She had a reputation as a tough lady. She sang in nightclubs, not the nightclubs we knew with white tablecloths, but dives and cellars, where you took your own bottle of drink. She had great respect as an artist but she didn't sing in smart places." At the same time, Elisabeth heard about Ethel's relationship with dancer Ethel Williams: "They were known as 'The Two Ethels' but I was very young and didn't know about les-ians. It was scandalous for two women to live together as a couple. The Ethel was light-skinned, skinny, and red-haired. She had no personal-ity at all. Ethel Waters was called a bull dyke, a terrible name. Most people knew they were lovers and we heard that they sometimes argued in public."[8]

There are a number of references to Ethel Williams in Ethel's 1951 auto-biography, and Waters's enthusiasm for Williams's talent is evident. Williams had a reputation as an exceptional dancer who specialized in the shimmy, and Waters describes her as a "truly gifted dancer" and "a brilliant performer," but she makes no mention of their relationship. Ethel's final reference to her lover is simple and direct: "Ethel Williams quit our act to marry Clarence Dotson, the dancer." Ethel Williams is described in the *New York Age* (June 3, 1922) as a dancer whose shimmies and shivers "sent the crowd into parox-ysms of the wildest delight." They describe her appearance as "almost white, with her form of a Venus and the eyes of a devil" and add that "she lifted the audience up and up until it literally overflowed with delight." Other than that, there is very little information available about her, though her name can be found in the cast of *The Gunsaulus Mystery* (1921), written and di-rected by pioneer black filmmaker Oscar Micheaux, as well as the 1922 stage show *Oh Joy!* in which she appeared with Ethel. In 1926 she is billed as "Ethel Williams Dotson" in the cast of *Mamie Smith Revue*, which indicates a possible time when her relationship with Ethel had ended and her marriage to the popular Clarence "Dancing" Dotson began. In 1930 she is listed in the cast of *Moanin' Low*, a revue starring Bessie Smith. She was still living in 1961 when Marshall and Jean Stearns interviewed her in New York for their book *Jazz Dance: The Story of Vernacular Dance*. In this pioneer work, they re-veal that Ethel Williams began her career as a child in 1897 and was given her first big break in the musical *Darktown Follies*, which opened at Harlem's Lafayette Theatre in 1913.

In 1984 the critically acclaimed documentary film *Before Stonewall* traced the evolution of the lesbian and gay movement in the United States from the 1920s to the 1960s, documenting from archive footage and memorable inter-views what it was like to be "in the life" during this period. The film embraces life in lesbian bars in Harlem in the 1920s, a gay soldier's experiences in the Second World War, and what it had been like for gay African Americans and

Native Americans. It took as its ending the 1969 Stonewall riots in New York, which gave birth to what is now recognized as the modern gay rights movement. The African Americans interviewed in *Before Stonewall* include Mabel Hampton. She reveals that Ethel, like her blues singing contemporaries Gertrude "Ma" Rainey, Bessie Smith, Alberta Hunter, and Gladys Bentley, were either lesbians or bisexuals: "They were *all* in the life. I wouldn't have been meeting them if they hadn't!"[9] Joan Nestle, a cofounder of New York's Lesbian Herstory Archives and historical consultant on *Before Stonewall*, reveals in a letter to me: "I can tell you from personal experience—my friendship and oral-history making with Mabel Hampton who knew Ethel Waters and her lover—that your phrase 'the two Ethels' was one Mabel used constantly in referring to her friends; she also implied that their relationship was a stormy one, full of passion and fights. You are the only other person I have heard use that phrase."[10]

The majority of lesbians and gays grew up in an era that did not permit discussion of sexuality, much less acceptance of homosexuality. For Alberta Hunter, the subject remained one she refused to discuss: "But she went further. Alberta did everything to conceal this preference all her life. In her mind lesbianism tarnished the image of propriety and respectability she struggled so hard to achieve."[11] Unlike Alberta, Gladys Bentley publicly exploited her lesbian identity, specializing in male impersonation and risqué songs. Langston Hughes describes her as

> something worth discovering in those days, before she got famous, acquired an accompanist, specially written material, and conscious vulgarity. But for two or three amazing years, Miss Bentley sat, and played a big piano all night long, literally all night, without stopping—singing songs like "St. James Infirmary," from ten in the evening until dawn, with scarcely a break between the notes, sliding from one song to another, with a powerful and continuous underbeat of jungle rhythm. Miss Bentley was an amazing exhibition of musical energy—a large, dark, masculine lady, whose feet pounded the floor while her fingers pounded the keyboard—a perfect piece of African sculpture, animated by her own rhythm.[12]

In *Queer Noises*, a study of homosexuality in twentieth-century music, John Gill says that "owing to the hypocrisy and homophobia of jazz writers (a criticism that is still being levelled by black gay critics in the mid-1990s) much queer blues history has been erased and lost forever. While individual stories have been censored or elided to gloss over details of oppositional sexuality, evidence exists to suggest that homosexuality was both commonplace in black society and an acceptable topic for musical treatment in the frequently ribald, and indeed lewd, world of the blues."[13]

Reflecting on African American women in the world of entertainment in the 1920s, Maude Russell, in a biography of Josephine Baker, explains why some of them were drawn into same-sex relationships: "Often we girls would share a room because of the cost. Well, many of us had been kind of abused by producers, directors, leading men—if they liked girls. In those days, men only had what they wanted, they didn't care about pleasing a girl. And girls needed tenderness, so we had girl friendships, the famous lady lovers, but lesbians weren't well accepted in show business, they were called bull dykers. I guess we were bisexual, is what you would call it today."[14]

Ethel and her contemporaries also enjoyed lesbian and gay followings, and one of Ethel's most devoted gay fans was Carl Van Vechten. In March 1926, Van Vechten published an essay in *Vanity Fair* titled "Negro Blues Singers," an appreciation of Bessie Smith, Clara Smith, and Ethel. He expresses a particular fondness for Ethel:

> If Bessie Smith is crude and primitive, she represents the true folk-spirit of the race. She sings Blues as they are understood and admired by the coloured masses. Of the artists who have communicated the Blues to the more sophisticated Negro and white public, I think Ethel Waters is the best. She refines her comedy, refines her pathos, refines even her obscenities. . . . She is a natural comedienne. . . . Some of her songs she croons; she never shouts. Her methods are precisely opposed to those of the crude coon shouter, to those of the authentic Blues singer, and yet, not for once, does she lose the veridical Negro atmosphere. Her voice and her gestures are essentially Negro, but they have been thought out and restrained, not prettified, but stylized.[15]

The publication of Van Vechten's controversial novel *Nigger Heaven* in 1926 upset Ethel. At first, she condemned the book without reading it, but after she read it, she thought it a sympathetic treatment of the way African Americans lived in Harlem. Van Vechten wanted to meet Ethel, but she was indifferent. White people bored her. But eventually Ethel and Van Vechten struck up a friendship, and in the 1930s, when he began taking portrait photographs, Ethel became one of his many subjects. Others include Gertrude Stein, F. Scott Fitzgerald, and Bessie Smith. Van Vechten told Ethel she was the only black person he'd ever met who was at ease and completely natural with him. Ethel responded by telling him he'd been hanging around mostly with "dictys" who tried to be as much like whites as possible! It was at the home of Van Vechten that Ethel met many famous celebrities. In her 1951 autobiography she mentions—in passing—other gay men such as Cole Porter, Noel Coward, and Somerset Maugham and that, in Harlem in the 1920s, she was popular with drag queens:

> That was the great time of "drags" in Harlem. In these affairs there would be fashion parades for the male queers dressed in women's clothes. They would beg me to let them wear my best gowns for the evening so they could compete for the grand prizes. And they did win many first prizes in my clothes. One night I lent my black velvet dress, trimmed with ermine, to one of these he-she-and-what-is-it types. But he got to fighting with his "husband" at the affair and was locked up in a cell. And with him to jail went my expensive black velvet dress trimmed with ermine. The dress smelled of carbolic acid, the Chanel No. 5 of the cell blocks, for months, and I couldn't wear it. I would not have been much more humiliated if I myself had been thrown into the poky.[16]

Ethel is rumored to have had an affair with lesbian novelist Radclyffe Hall. They met in Paris around 1929, and Ethel briefly recalls this encounter in her 1951 autobiography: "I met a lot of people in Paris, and Radclyffe Hall, the author of *The Well of Loneliness*, was the most interesting of them." But, says Michael Baker, the author of a biography of Hall called *Our Three Selves*,

> I am afraid that I never came across any mention of Ethel Waters in my researches for the Radclyffe Hall biography. I would be sceptical of any claims that they had an affair, principally, I think, because Ethel was black. I say this because Radclyffe Hall's choice of lovers tended to be strictly "conventional"—in the sense that they were largely drawn from a white, middle-to-upper class British or American peer group. It's true that Souline, her last great passion, was a working nurse of Slavic origins (she had "Chinky" features, according to RH, and her family were supposedly White Russians), but this seems to have been a bit of "rough" that proved the exception to the rule. Certainly in the 1930s, indeed right up to the first years of the war, RH supported Mussolini and, like many upper-class Britishers, resented Jews and "foreigners." She was not therefore, I suppose, very likely to take a black entertainer as a lover. But, in truth, there's no evidence either way.[17]

Ethel's relationships with men were disastrous. They were also childless, though for a short time in the late 1920s and early 1930s she did foster Algretta, the young daughter of a friend. Before her relationship with Ethel Williams, there had been her first husband, Merritt "Buddy" Purnsley. Ethel married him in 1910 when she was just thirteen (even though the minimum age for marriage in Pennsylvania was eighteen), and he was almost twice her age. Ethel described her wedding night as nasty and unpleasant. Thereafter "Buddy" cheated on her and beat her. At fourteen, Ethel ended the marriage. In 1928, after her relationship with Ethel Williams had run its course, Ethel married her second husband, Clyde Edward Matthews, known as "Eddie," but that marriage didn't last either. In 1933 Ethel dumped him during the run of her Broadway hit *As Thousands Cheer*. In 1935, while working on Broadway in *At Home Abroad*, a trumpet player called Eddie Mallory attracted her attention. Ethel made him husband number three, financed a big band for him, and traveled with the band for several years; in 1938–1939 they made a number of recordings on the Bluebird label. These include an impressive version of "Frankie and Johnny." The marriage to Mallory also ended in tears in the early 1940s.

Interviewed in the 1990s, Elisabeth Welch summarizes how Ethel's sexual preferences altered throughout her life. At first she was a lesbian, but "after she became famous, Ethel turned the other way, but her relationships with men were disastrous. They abused and exploited her. Eventually she turned her back on men, took up religion, and preached the word of God till the day she died. She ended up with that man, Billy Graham, the evangelist, singing hymns and gathering flock for Jesus."[18]

Notes

1. Stephen Bourne, *Elisabeth Welch: Soft Lights and Sweet Music* (Lanham, Md.: Scarecrow Press, 2005), 15.

2. Bricktop with James Haskins, *Bricktop* (New York: Atheneum, 1983), 183.

3. Marian Anderson, *My Lord, What a Morning* (Cresset Press: London, 1957), 103.

4. Martin Bauml Duberman, *Paul Robeson* (London: Bodley Head, 1989), 49.

5. Howard Rye, "Visiting Firemen 12," *Storyville* 126 (August/September 1986), 219–22.

6. Ethel Waters with Charles Samuels, *His Eye Is on the Sparrow* (New York: Da Capo, 1992), 211.

7. Bruce Kellner, ed., *Letters of Carl Van Vechten* (New Haven: Yale University Press, 1987), 129.

8. Bourne, *Elisabeth Welch*, 14–15.

9. Mabel Hampton, interviewed in the 1984 documentary *Before Stonewall: The Making of a Gay and Lesbian Community*.

10. Joan Nestle, letter to Stephen Bourne, February 10, 1994. Reproduced with permission.

11. Frank C. Taylor and Gerald Cook, *Alberta Hunter: A Celebration in Blues* (New York: McGraw-Hill, 1987), 42–43.

12. Langston Hughes, *The Big Sea: An Autobiography* (New York: Knopf, 1940), 226.

13. John Gill, *Queer Noises: Male and Female Homosexuality in Twentieth-Century Music* (London: Cassell, 1995), 42.

14. Jean-Claude Baker and Chris Chase, *Josephine: The Hungry Heart* (Holbrook, Mass.: Adams 1993), 63–64.

15. Carl Van Vechten, "Negro Blues Singers," *Vanity Fair* 26, no. 1 (March 1926), 106.

16. Waters, *Sparrow*, 149–50.

17. Michael Baker, letter to Stephen Bourne, November 10, 1993. Reproduced with permission.

18. Bourne, *Elisabeth Welch*, 15.

CHAPTER FOUR

~

The Cotton Club and "Stormy Weather"

The Harlem Renaissance of the 1920s was a large-scale explosion of creative energy and artistic expression from African American artists and intellectuals. Stage musicals and revues, as well as nightclubs such as the Cotton Club (formerly the Club Deluxe), showcased black talent, and African American performers enjoyed unprecedented success and popularity in white and urban black America. Heavyweight champion Jack Johnson opened the Club Deluxe at 142nd Street and Lenox Avenue in Harlem in 1920. A prominent bootlegger and gangster named Owney Madden took over the club in 1923 while he was imprisoned in Sing Sing. It was Madden who changed its name to the Cotton Club. It was a fashionable hot spot featuring top black entertainment for rich white-only audiences, and some of the many white celebrities who went there were the glamorous stars of Broadway and Hollywood: Tallulah Bankhead, Charlie Chaplin, Greta Garbo, Al Jolson, Harold Lloyd, the Marx Brothers, and Gloria Swanson. The Club's cabaret shows attracted the most famous African American stars around: Duke Ellington (from 1927 to 1931, and occasionally thereafter), Bill Robinson, Cab Calloway, Earl "Snakehips" Tucker, Jimmie Lunceford, the Nicholas Brothers, and Peg Leg Bates. Adelaide Hall, the star attraction of the 1934 *Cotton Club Parade* comments:

> The Cotton Club was a first class engagement. It was the most famous jazz club in America. It was an important place for black entertainers to be seen and an appearance there helped us to get on in the business. We knew that the place

was being run by gangsters, but we never got close to them. Sure, we heard about the stuff that went on when people didn't pay their bills, or when other clubs didn't keep to the rules enforced by the underworld, but we were never allowed to see anything like that. The underworld people who ran the Cotton Club were as nice and polite as you could imagine. They never gave us, the performers, any trouble at all. So we all stayed, and we worked . . . we were treated well. We could order any food we wanted and our salaries were paid on time. We weren't friends with the gangsters who owned the Club, but we weren't their enemies either.[1]

The Cotton Club was a small place, and the owners wanted the cabaret area to be as big as possible. Consequently, backstage the conditions were very bad. There was no space for dressing rooms, so the artistes were forced into a small, cramped area with just one curtain to separate the men and women. According to Adelaide, "We worked under those terrible conditions but there was nothing we could do about it. If we had complained about the conditions backstage we would have been fired. Also, because gangsters were running the Club, we didn't make a fuss. You can imagine what they would have done to us!"[2] The club was situated in Harlem, but black people were not allowed to sit out front and watch a cabaret with white patrons unless they were famous celebrities such as Bill Robinson. Occasionally light-skinned blacks were allowed in, and these included Elisabeth Welch. She was taken to the club by her older brother Eddie: "We went to the smart place, the Cotton Club, up in Harlem, to hear Cab Calloway. Eddie gave me my first drink at the Club. It was port. 'You have this for communion anyhow,' he said. The smart whites were in the audience and occasionally they accepted light-skinned Negroes. That's why Eddie and I were allowed in."'[3]
The club promoted the racist imagery of the times, often depicting blacks as savages in exotic jungles or as "darkies" on a plantation in the Deep South. A color bar was imposed on the chorus girls, whom the club presented in skimpy outfits. They were expected to be "tall, tan, and terrific," which meant they had to be at least five feet six inches tall, light skinned, and under twenty-one years of age. Elisabeth recalls: "The chorus girls were so beautiful, what we called 'high yellow' then. You had to be very pale to work in the Cotton Club. Some of the girls were blonde, genuine blonde, and with blue or grey eyes. The comedians and the male dancers could be dark-skinned but not the girls."[4] The club helped launch the career of Duke Ellington, whose orchestra was the house band there for several years. The club not only gave Ellington national exposure through radio broadcasts originating there but also enabled him to develop his repertoire as a composer.

In the Cotton Club chorus of 1934 was a beautiful sixteen-year-old named Lena Horne, who later said the following:

> Nostalgia has not played anyone false about the Cotton Club shows. They were wonderful. But for the employees, it was an exploitative system. . . . The club got great talent very cheap, because there were so few places for great Negro performers to work. . . . As for the "exotic," wonderful, rhythmic happy-go-lucky quality of our lives, that was a real joke. Especially for my family. We lived in a typical, roach-infested tenement.[5]

In 1933 Ethel accepted a lucrative offer to perform at the Cotton Club for the highest salary they had paid any other star. Composer Harold Arlen and lyricist Ted Koehler had written a superb new torch song for Ethel to sing in the twenty-second edition of the *Cotton Club Parade*, staged and produced by Dan Healy. It was called "Stormy Weather," and the song proved to be a turning point in her life. Neither Arlen nor Koehler remembered how they became associated with the Cotton Club. They wrote music for the club from 1930 to 1934, contributing hit songs to two shows a year. The songs they wrote for the club's 1931 show, *Rhythmania*, such as "Between the Devil and the Deep Blue Sea," became instant sensations. For the twenty-first edition of the Cotton Club revues in 1932, the first of the *Cotton Club Parades*, Arlen and Koehler made a splash with their new songs "I've Got the World on a String" and "Minnie the Moocher's Wedding Day," which was a specialty number for Cab Calloway as a follow-up to his hit song "Minnie The Moocher." Arlen was an innovative composer who— after working at the Cotton Club—contributed to the scores of several black Broadway musicals, including *St. Louis Woman* (1946); *House of Flowers* (1954), starring Pearl Bailey; and *Jamaica* (1957), starring Lena Horne and featuring Adelaide Hall. He also wrote the music for a number of Hollywood films, including two classic Judy Garland musicals: *The Wizard of Oz* and *A Star Is Born*. In Hollywood, in 1943, Arlen composed the music for Ethel's hit "Happiness Is a Thing Called Joe" (lyrics by E. Y. Harburg), which she performed in the film version of *Cabin in the Sky* (see chapter 6).

Arlen and Koehler created "Stormy Weather" with Cab Calloway in mind, but Calloway had not been signed to appear in the twenty-second edition of the *Parade*; Duke Ellington had been signed instead. So Ethel was invited to sing "Stormy Weather" with the Ellington orchestra. Arlen and Koehler believed she would be the perfect interpreter of their song. Ethel had only recently returned to New York from Chicago and Cicero, then Al Capone territory. Her career was at a standstill, and her personal life had hit another low point because her marriage to Eddie Matthews was breaking up.

"She listened with interest to Arlen and Koehler when they called upon her to talk about her appearing at the Cotton Club. Dan Healy had once devoted to the great singer an 'Ethel Waters Night,' which had made a favourable impression on her; besides, *her* friends, at least, were allowed in the Cotton Club. But Miss Waters agreed to appear . . . mainly because of the impact on her of 'Stormy Weather.'"[6] An RCA Victor recording of "Stormy Weather"—made in February 1933 and performed by the Leo Reisman Orchestra—generated such an interest in the song that by April 16, the opening night of the 1933 *Cotton Club Parade*, crowds of New York's elite gathered just to hear Ethel sing it:

> Not until the eleventh scene did the star, Miss Waters, appear. The scene was titled "Cabin in the Cotton Club." Healy had staged it simply against a log-cabin backdrop; Miss Waters stood under a lamppost, a midnight-blue spot on her, as she sang "Stormy Weather." After her chorus the scene imperceptively faded into the next as she was joined by George Dewey Washington, singing responses to Miss Waters' choruses; the Talbert choir joined them. By using special lights Healy was able to fade the girls practically unseen onto the dance floor. The transition from song to dance was done smoothly and effectively. The number stopped the show. On opening night, Healy remembers, there were at least a dozen encores.[7]

Drummer Sonny Greer, who was a member of Ellington's band from 1924 to 1951, later recalled that Ethel was "very hard to get along with. She didn't take no back-talk off nobody. I got along with her because when she started to get tight with me, I would dummy up and say nothing. You had to know how to handle her and stay a little ahead of her. And she sang 'Stormy Weather' like nobody."[8]

The "Stormy Weather Show," as the 1933 *Parade* came to be known, was one of the most successful ever staged at the Cotton Club. Ethel singing "Stormy Weather" became the talk of New York, and the message was carried by the newspaper columnists as well as by word of mouth, specifically by such celebrities as Jimmy Durante, Milton Berle, Lillian Roth, Eleanor Holm, George Raft, Ray Bolger, and Bert Lahr. People who rarely went to night clubs did so now. People who had never before visited the Cotton Club came to see Ethel. Irving Berlin did not often visit New York's cabarets, but he traveled to Harlem to hear Ethel sing "Stormy Weather," and it practically launched a new career for her. The day after he saw the show, Berlin called Healy, offering to buy out Miss Waters's contract (a nonexistent document). Berlin wanted her to appear in his new Broadway revue *As Thousands Cheer,* which was about to go into rehearsal (see chapter 5). Ethel would always credit "Stormy Weather" as the turning point in her career.

Ethel recorded "Stormy Weather" on May 3 for Columbia, and this became Ethel's next crossover hit, a success even larger than "Dinah." For Ethel, "Stormy Weather" was "the perfect expression of my mood, and I found release in singing it each evening. When I got out there in the middle of the Cotton Club floor I was telling the things I couldn't frame in words. I was singing the story of my misery and confusion, of the misunderstandings in my life I couldn't straighten out, the story of the wrongs and outrages done to me by people I had loved and trusted. . . . I sang 'Stormy Weather' from the depths of the private hell in which I was being crushed and suffocated."[9]

Lena Horne was just a kid when she began her long and successful career at the Cotton Club. According to Adelaide Hall, "her mother accompanied her to the club every night as her chaperone."[10] Legend has it that, in her effort to study the styles of successful singers, young Lena would entertain the other chorines with her impressions, and Jim Haskins claims that one of her best was of Ethel singing "Stormy Weather": "The story goes that one night in her own dressing room she [Ethel] heard Lena imitating her. She walked into the chorus girls' dressing room, much to Lena's embarrassment. 'It was just in fun, Miss Waters,' she is supposed to have mumbled. 'In fun, girl?' Ethel cried. 'That's fine singing. You get busy and don't let anybody stop you from singing from now on.'"[11] However, though it's a great story, it's probably fiction, unless it happened somewhere else, at a benefit perhaps, not the Cotton Club, because Lena did not make her first appearance at the Cotton Club until Adelaide Hall's 1934 show, the year *after* Ethel had headlined there. Lena's daughter Gail confirmed this in an e-mail I received on September 5, 2006: "Mother says that her first show starred Adelaide. Ethel was a giant. My mother idolized her as a huge star long before *Cabin in the Sky* and did a 'modern dance' at a charity recital to 'Stormy Weather' just before she went into the Cotton Club. Hope this is of help."

The Cotton Club closed in February 1936, after the race riot in Harlem the previous year, and reopened later that year—in September—at Broadway and 48th Street, near Times Square. It closed for good in 1940, under pressure from higher rents, changing tastes, and a federal investigation into tax evasion by Manhattan nightclub owners. In 1937 (March 17 to June 15), Ethel and Duke Ellington returned to the reopened club for the *Cotton Club Express*, which also featured the Nicholas Brothers: "We called her Miss Waters and she was a great star, one of the biggest in the United States. We heard that she could be temperamental, but we never had any trouble with her. She was always nice to us."[12] The 1937 show was a great success and included many important numbers written by black composers and lyricists, such as Ellington, Andy Razaf, and John Redmond. Even Britain's brilliant jazz innovator Reginald Foresythe got in on the act. Ethel's big show stopper was Redmond and Lee David's "Where is the Sun?" and she also revived some of her old hits, including "Stormy Weather." An unidentified columnist, quoted in Jim Haskins's book *The Cotton Club* (1977), raves:

> When you encounter her striking interpretations of some songs ranging from her classic "Stormy Weather" to Cole Porter's sardonic "Miss Otis Regrets," you will see that she is, among other things, a truly creative player. She dominates the performance, dominates it with her unflagging spirit, her casual splendour and her instinctive theatrical wisdom, and I suspect that, even without the other virtues of the evening, she, splendidly accompanied by her brother [Johnny Waters] on the piano and her husband [Eddie Mallory] on a muted cornet, would revive for you all the glories of a fine tradition. . . . The show was a smash—lively, fast-paced and, to quote Ed Sullivan, "easily the most elegant colored show Broadway has ever applauded."[13]

"Stormy Weather" was introduced to Britain when Elisabeth Welch made her London stage debut on June 26, 1933, in a revue at the Leicester Square Theatre. She had already featured the song in her cabaret act in Paris, where she made a recording of the song sometime in May or June 1933. In Britain, the song became forever associated with Elisabeth, who kept it in her repertoire until she retired in the early 1990s. In the 1930s the song was associated with several other African American female vocalists, including Ivie Anderson, who performed it with the Duke Ellington orchestra, and Adelaide Hall. They all helped make "Stormy Weather" an international hit. It was later recorded by many of the great popular singers of the century, including Frank Sinatra, Billie Holiday, and Judy Garland in her famous Carnegie Hall concert in 1961. When Lena Horne sang it in the Hollywood movie *Stormy Weather* (1943), the song became closely associated with her, more than with Ethel. It became an important feature of her act, including her award-winning one-woman Broadway show *The Lady and Her Music* (1981). In 2000 it was Lena's 1942 recording of "Stormy Weather" on the RCA Victor label that was inducted into the Grammy Hall of Fame in the category of Traditional Pop (Single). Two years earlier Ethel's 1925 version of "Dinah" had been inducted, but it seemed incredible that her version of "Stormy Weather" was missing from the Hall of Fame. Finally, in 2003, seventy years after she had made her recording, the Grammy Hall of Fame acknowledged Ethel's influential version of the song in the Jazz (Single) category.

Notes

1. Stephen Bourne, *Sophisticated Lady: A Celebration of Adelaide Hall* (London: ECOHP, 2001), 22.

2. Bourne, *Sophisticated Lady*, 23.

3. Stephen Bourne, *Elisabeth Welch: Soft Lights and Sweet Music* (Lanham, Md.: Scarecrow Press, 2005), 9.

4. Bourne, *Elisabeth Welch*, 9.

5. Lena Horne with Richard Schickel, *Lena* (London: Deutsch, 1966), 53–55.

6. Edward Jablonski, *Harold Arlen: Happy with the Blues* (New York: Doubleday, 1961), 62.

7. Jablonski, *Harold Arlen*, 63–64.

8. Stuart Nicholson, *A Portrait of Duke Ellington: Reminiscing in Tempo* (London: Sidgwick and Jackson, 1999), 128.

9. Ethel Waters with Charles Samuels, *His Eye Is on the Sparrow* (New York: Da Capo, 1992), 220.

10. Bourne, *Sophisticated Lady*, 22.

11. Jim Haskins, *The Cotton Club* (London: Robson, 1985), 95.

12. Fayard and Harold Nicholas, interview with Stephen Bourne, London, June 1, 1990.

13. Undated newspaper clipping in the Lincoln Center for the Performing Arts Library, quoted in Haskins, *The Cotton Club*, 123–24.

CHAPTER FIVE

~

Back on Broadway

Composer and lyricist Irving Berlin had been impressed with Ethel when he saw her in the short-lived Broadway revue *Africana* (1927). He was impressed once more when he attended a performance of "Stormy Weather" at the Cotton Club. Berlin was determined to feature her in his Broadway revue *As Thousands Cheer*, but racism prevented black performers from appearing on the Great White Way in integrated casts unless they played servants. Before Ethel was cast in *As Thousands Cheer*, comedian Bert Williams was one of the first black men to be integrated into white shows when he costarred in *Ziegfeld Follies* (1910–1919), but only two black women had been integrated into "white" Broadway revues: Florence Mills (*Greenwich Village Follies*, 1923) and Elisabeth Welch (*The New Yorkers*, 1931). In fact, it was Berlin who had been responsible for Elisabeth being cast. A "pink and white" blonde girl, who looked like a schoolgirl, had been singing Cole Porter's "Love for Sale," a prostitute's lament, in *The New Yorkers*. Totally unsuitable for such a number, the critics slated. Porter left for Paris in a rage three days after the show opened. The "pink and white" singer had to be replaced, and it was decided that white audiences—and critics—would be less offended if a black singer was cast as the streetwalker. Consequently the revue's director, Monty Woolley, and its producer, E. Ray Goetz, teamed up with Irving Berlin and auditioned Elisabeth, who was then working in cabaret in New York, but Goetz expressed some concern about putting a black singer in the show. "That's no obstacle," said Berlin, "She's a wonderful singer and if you want her in the show you can always find the right spot for her."[1] Clearly, Berlin was more interested in promoting talent than com-

39

plying with Broadway's racist taboos. In Paris, Porter gave his consent, and Elisabeth joined the cast in January 1931. She later acknowledged this as the turning point in her career.

Opening at the Music Box Theatre on September 30, 1933, *As Thousands Cheer* had a strikingly original format: It was designed in the form of a newspaper, with every song, dance, and sketch intended to illustrate a current event or feature. Real names of famous people were used. Critic Margo Jefferson explains in the television documentary *Broadway: The American Musical* (2004) that "the revue which had been very light and entertaining through the twenties was becoming sharp and politically aware and Irving Berlin had decided fittingly—given the thirties and this political consciousness that was making its way into popular entertainment—that he wanted to do a timely revue."[2] Stanley Green describes *As Thousands Cheer* as one of the most successful Broadway revues of the 1930s, running for 400 performances:

> With music and lyrics by Irving Berlin and sketches by Moss Hart, it was created in the form of a newspaper, with songs and sketches representing various sections. All dealt with their themes in a light, satirical fashion except for the dramatic "Supper Time." . . . Berlin was urged to cut the number from the show, but, as he put it, "I was convinced that a musical dealing with headline news needed at least one serious piece, and I knew that Ethel Waters had the quality to sing something really dramatic."[3]

Producer Sam H. Harris was not so daring when it came to billing. He would only give Ethel featured billing below his three white stars: Marilyn Miller, Clifton Webb, and Helen Broderick. However, Berlin gave Ethel three sensational numbers to sing: "Heat Wave," "Supper Time," and "Harlem on My Mind." Says Laurence Bergreen in his biography of Berlin:

> Although the audience came to see Marilyn Miller, Ethel Waters nearly stole the show because each song Berlin had written for her was a gem. As the headline "HEAT WAVE HITS NEW YORK" appeared, she launched into her torch song, "Heat Wave." When another headline told of mob violence in the South—"UNKNOWN NEGRO LYNCHED BY FRENZIED MOB"—she displayed her dramatic range in "Supper Time," the magnificently understated lament of the wife of the victim, who must tell her children that they will never see their father again. This was a tragic strain, to be sure, but by no means a protest song. Berlin had so personalized and muted the incendiary racial aspects of the event that what the song lost in bite it gained in universality.
>
> Berlin gave Waters one other song, the sultry "Harlem on My Mind," in which he attempted to anatomize in musical terms what he perceived as the

split personality of the American Black. For the number, Waters adopted the persona of a rakehell black expatriate in Paris (similar to Josephine Baker) who yearns for home even at the risk of degradation while she exults in her newly acquired European sophistication.[4]

The setting for "Supper Time" was stark. The brick wall on the back of the theatre was the set, and Ethel Waters's entrance was shocking, as legendary Broadway star Carol Channing recalls in *Broadway: The American Musical*: "This monumental woman had a bandanna on her head, she had an apron on, but behind her was the silhouette of a man hanging from a tree with his head on his side, with the rope around his neck. We didn't know in those days about lynchings in the South. She came forward with the beat of that orchestra and she went into 'Supper Time.'"[5] Ethel remarks: "When people praise my 'marvellous acting ability,' they don't know that when I used to sing 'Supper Time' in *As Thousands Cheer* and later in my one-woman shows, I was reliving the agony I shared with a Southern colored family whose beloved son had been lynched, and the time I was almost lynched once myself in Georgia a long time ago, by a theater operator who wanted me out of his way."[6]

As Thousands Cheer was a smash hit. Everyone wanted to see it, even when Miller and Webb took off for the summer (of 1934), and Ethel received star billing for the first time with Helen Broderick. Ethel's casting in *As Thousands Cheer* helped her career enormously. It transformed her into the highest-paid woman on Broadway, and her appearance broke down a racial barrier that had existed on Broadway for years. According to theatre historian Max Wilk in *Broadway: The American Musical*, "the tradition was that black performers should stay in vaudeville or they should stay in minstrel shows but they don't mix the two races."[7] Even so, Ethel was not allowed to appear on stage with her white costars in any sketches or songs. As a black artiste she was carefully segregated in an integrated show. She was also subjected to racism from her white costars before the show opened on Broadway, an incident Berlin took very seriously. His daughter, Mary, was seven years old when he took her to see *As Thousands Cheer* in December 1933. She reveals in *Irving Berlin: A Daughter's Memoir* that Ethel was her favorite member of the cast and that, in Philadelphia, "Marilyn Miller, Clifton Webb, and Helen Broderick refused to take a bow with Ethel Waters, she being black and they white. He would respect their feelings, of course, my father had said, only in that case there need be no bows at all. The next night, Mr. Webb, Miss Miller and Miss Broderick took their bows with Miss Waters. . . . The curtain-call story had to do with color and color blindness. But I liked to give it another interpretation. 'They must have been jealous,' I said. 'She was the best.'"8

Opening at the Winter Garden Theatre on September 19, 1935, *At Home Abroad* was subtitled "A Musical Holiday" because the setting was a world cruise, though it carefully avoided such countries as Germany, Italy, and Russia. One of the highlights of this revue was comedienne Beatrice Lillie and her classic tongue-twisting sketch about ordering two dozen double-damask dinner napkins in a London department store. The show also provided Ethel with her second costarring role with white artists on Broadway, but it was generally agreed that her material was not in the same league as Berlin's *As Thousands Cheer*. Arthur Schwartz (music) and Howard Dietz (lyrics) wrote several numbers for Ethel, who played several roles. These included a Harlem lady who lectured the natives of the Congo on her position as a "Hottentot Potentate." She also sang "Thief in the Night," "Loadin' Time" (in a West Indies setting), and duetted on "Got a Bran' New Suit" with the great tap dancer Eleanor Powell, who then found fame in Hollywood.

At Home Abroad ran for 198 performances, and it was the first complete Broadway musical to be directed by Vincente Minnelli, who later reflected: "No huge hits came out of *At Home Abroad*, but the songs worked well within their context."9 In 1938 Minnelli worked on a treatment for a musical version of *Serena Blandish*, the S. N. Behrman play adapted from Enid Bagnold's *A Lady of Quality*. He planned to feature Ethel and Lena Horne in this tantalizing production because he wanted to do a "sophisticated black show." Minnelli said he felt "uneasy about the conventional stereotype of the Negro as simple, naïve, and childlike." In Minnelli's version, Lena would star as Serena, who is loaned a diamond for a month by a jeweler and introduced to society by Countess Flor di Folio, an Auntie Mame character, played by Ethel. Cole Porter was approached to write the songs. According to Minnelli, "Negotiations for large productions rarely run smoothly, and the wheeling and dealing for *Serena* had been rockier than most. . . . I worked into 1939 trying to find a way to do the show. Unfortunately I couldn't. Neither could anyone else. After six months on the project, I regretfully admitted defeat."10 A few years later, Minnelli was finally given an opportunity to work with Lena and Ethel when he directed them in MGM's screen version of the Broadway hit *Cabin in the Sky* (see chapter 6).

In 1939 Ethel captivated Broadway in *Mamba's Daughters*, her first dramatic role, and she made history by becoming the first black actress to receive top billing in a play. Opening on January 3, *Mamba's Daughters* was the first play with a predominantly black cast to be presented at the Empire Theatre in New York. It was set in Catfish Row in Charleston, South Carolina.

Ethel was cast as Hagar, who tries to give her daughter Lissa (Fredi Washington) all the opportunities she didn't have when growing up. When a blackmailer threatens Lissa's successful singing career, Hagar strangles him to death. She hears Lissa singing on the radio, then kills herself. Other African American women in the cast included Georgette Harvey as Mamba (Hagar's mother) and Alberta Hunter. Ethel comments: "Even when I read it for the first time I understood instinctively that there could be no greater triumph in my professional career than playing Hagar. All my life I'd burned to tell the story of my mother's despair and long defeat."[11]

This play was a breakthrough for African American women in the performing arts. The same year, on Easter Sunday, contralto Marian Anderson was forced to sing on the steps of the Lincoln Memorial in Washington D.C. The Daughters of the American Revolution (DAR) had refused to allow Anderson to sing to an integrated audience in Constitution Hall because of her race. As a result of the controversy that followed, thousands of DAR members, including the president's wife, Eleanor Roosevelt, resigned, and the Lincoln Memorial concert was organized. Until Ethel's breakthrough, black actresses had rarely been given opportunities to perform in dramatic productions, unless they played maids, though some, such as Rose McClendon, had attained recognition. McClendon (1884–1936) had been called the "Negro first lady of the dramatic stage," primarily for her roles in *In Abraham's Bosom* (1926), *Porgy* (1927), and Langston Hughes's *Mulatto* (1935). It would take until 2004 for a black leading lady in a dramatic role to win a Tony (Broadway's equivalent of the Oscar), when Phylicia Rashad was honored as best actress in a play for her portrayal of Lena Younger in the revival of Lorraine Hansberry's *A Raisin in the Sun* at the Royale, the same theatre where Ethel had performed in *Lew Leslie's Blackbirds* in 1930.

Mamba's Daughters had been written for Ethel by DuBose Heyward and his wife, Dorothy. It was based on his 1929 novel, two years after their play *Porgy* had opened to acclaim on Broadway. The Heywards had taken a stand on Broadway by insisting that black actors be cast in *Porgy*, not white actors in blackface. When the Heywards dramatized *Mamba's Daughters*, they obliterated most of the white characters from the novel, giving the drama over to the black family. The play had been written expressly with Ethel in mind after they had met her in New York in 1935, soon after the opening of George Gershwin's folk opera *Porgy and Bess*. Ethel had been invited to a party given by her friend, Georgette Harvey, who had sung Maria in the opera. The Heywards were there, too, and Ethel happened to be sitting with them on a couch, unaware of who they were. After Ethel criticized *Porgy*, Dorothy delicately made it clear that Ethel was talking to the author, DuBose, so Ethel changed the subject to *Mamba's Daughters*, not knowing that DuBose had written that novel:

> She had been struck by how much Mamba's family was like her own, she told them, but of the three generations of the story it was Mamba's daughter Hagar who had impressed her as the book's most important character, much like her own mother, and like "all Negro women lost and lonely in the white man's antagonistic world." The astute Dorothy Heyward mentioned that her husband had written the novel and then promised Ethel Waters that if they were to dramatise the novel she would have the first chance at the lead. Two years later the play was written and they sent the script to her. She not only agreed to play the role of Hagar, around which the story was now built, but refused other commitments that would tie her up if a production was imminent. . . . Getting the play onstage, though, was difficult. The Theatre Guild turned it down, as did several other producers. Some felt the play was too melodramatic; others did not think Ethel Waters—on whom the Heywards were insistent—was accomplished enough as an actress to carry it. Frustrated by his inability to get the play produced, Heyward took it to a friend, Guthrie McClintic, the director husband of Katharine Cornell, for an opinion. McClintic not only agreed to put the play on his schedule, but championed Ethel Waters for the key role of a strong, devoted, generous woman, yet one capable of the violent rage which would cause her to kill the vicious seducer of her daughter, Lissa (changed from an opera singer to a radio vocalist).[12]

Ethel was thrilled to have the Empire Theatre's star dressing room on opening night: "I sat at the dressing table where all the great actresses, past and present, had sat as they made up their faces and wondered what the first-night verdict would be—Maud Adams, Ethel Barrymore, Helen Hayes, Katharine Cornell, Lynn Fontanne . . . who had brought the glitter of talent and beauty and grace to that old stage. . . . That was *the* night of my professional life, sitting there in that old-fashioned dressing room. . . . The night I'd been born for, and God was in the room with me. I talked to God until the callboy came to say: 'Five minutes, Miss Waters.'"[13]

Ethel received seventeen curtain calls that opening night, and Rosetta LeNoire, who in the 1960s became the director of the African American AMAS Repertory Theatre in New York, attended the opening night. She recalls, "I'll never forget that night. They took I don't know how many curtain calls. Finally Ethel Waters just stood there with the company all bowing their heads and the tears came down their faces. Then the house went wild."[14]

Ethel had accomplished what actresses such as Rose McClendon had struggled hard to achieve: the establishment of a black actress as a major force on the

American stage. The play itself received mixed reviews, but with the exception of Brooks Atkinson in the *New York Times*, critics were unanimous in their praise of Ethel's magnificent performance. Angered by Atkinson's negative review, Carl Van Vechten and eighteen friends from the world of theatre, including Judith Anderson, Tallulah Bankhead, Dorothy Gish, Oscar Hammerstein II, Aline MacMahon, and Burgess Meredith, paid for an ad in the *New York Times* (January 6, 1939) to rebuke Atkinson. It read: "We the undersigned feel that Ethel Waters' superb performance in *Mamba's Daughters* . . . is a profound emotional experience which any playgoer would be the poorer for missing. It seems to be such a magnificent example of great acting, simple, deeply felt, moving on a plane of complete reality that we are glad to pay for the privilege of saying so." Atkinson, not known for retracting his views, went back to see the play and changed his mind about it and Ethel. He informed his readers that the first time he saw the play he had the flu.

The Broadway production closed on May 20, 1939, after 162 performances, in preparation for a tour that opened on October 2 at Chicago's Grand Opera House. After the tour, *Mamba's Daughters* returned to Broadway on March 23, 1940, for a second engagement, this time at the Broadway Theatre. However, due to union problems, the run was cut short and closed after seventeen performances on April 6. Meanwhile, Ethel, Fredi Washington, and Georgette Harvey took part in a historic experimental telecast for NBC on June 14, 1939, in a scene from *Mamba's Daughters* (see chapter 10), and on March 18, 1951, Ethel enacted Hagar once more for an excerpt from the play in NBC's popular radio program *The Big Show*, hosted by Tallulah Bankhead.

Ethel's relationships with her costars could be stormy, but they could also be rewarding. During *Mamba's Daughters* she worked with two African American actresses, Alberta Hunter and Frances E. Williams, and they have offered fascinating insights into her complex personality. Alberta reveals that, during the Broadway production, Ethel gave her a hard time: "She treated me like a dog. Fine artist, but, oh, she was so mean. . . . Later she wrote me a letter asking my forgiveness. She knew she was wrong. She couldn't help it. That was just her disposition. It was professional jealousy. I don't think she meant any harm. She didn't hate me as a person."[15]

Frances had first met Ethel in New York some years prior to the Broadway production, and they renewed their friendship in 1939:

Ethel was getting ready to do a tour of the play *Mamba's Daughters*. We went down to see them rehearse and at one point she said to me, "I don't have anything decent to wear in the way of costumes. Look in that wardrobe and see if you can help me." I helped her piece together something half-way decent, at any rate, from this disastrous grab bag of shrunken, wadded-up costumes, and she was so grateful that she said, "Why don't you go up the coast with me and be my understudy?" I did and we got to become good friends fairly quickly, but even after that I'd sometimes look up and see her looking at me in this funny way, like she was still trying to figure out if I might really be an enemy. She'd been really roughed up coming up in show business . . . and she just couldn't bring herself to trust people very much. But she was really very kind, generous and loyal . . . and perceptive. I loved her dearly.[16]

Notes

1. Stephen Bourne, *Elisabeth Welch: Soft Lights and Sweet Music* (Lanham, Md.: Scarecrow Press, 2005), 24.

2. Margo Jefferson, *Broadway: The American Musical* (2004), directed by Michael Kantor, a six-part television documentary about the American musical.

3. Stanley Green, *Encyclopedia of the Musical* (London: Cassell, 1976), 408.

4. Laurence Bergreen, *As Thousands Cheer: The Life of Irving Berlin* (London: Hodder and Stoughton, 1990), 321–22.

5. Carol Channing, *Broadway: The American Musical.*

6. Ethel Waters, *To Me It's Wonderful* (New York: Harper and Row, 1972), 135.

7. Max Wilk, *Broadway: The American Musical.*

8. Mary Ellin Barrett, *Irving Berlin: A Daughter's Memoir* (London: Simon and Schuster, 1995), 120–21.

9. Vincente Minnelli with Hector Arce, *I Remember It Well* (London: Angus and Robertson, 1975), 70–71.

10. Minnelli, *I Remember*, 103–6.

11. Ethel Waters with Charles Samuels, *His Eye Is on the Sparrow* (New York: Da Capo, 1992), 239.

12. Hollis Alpert, *The Life and Times of Porgy and Bess: The Story of an American Classic* (London: Hern, 1990), 132–33.

13. Waters, *Sparrow*, 247.

14. Frank C. Taylor and Gerald Cook, *Alberta Hunter: A Celebration in Blues* (New York: McGraw-Hill, 1987), 143.

15. Taylor and Cook, *Alberta Hunter*, 147.

16. Bill Reed, *Hot from Harlem: Profiles in Classic African-American Entertainment* (Los Angeles: Cellar Door, 1998), 200–201.

CHAPTER SIX

~

Cabin in the Sky

After the musical *Cabin in the Sky* opened on Broadway on October 25, 1940, a small group of leading ladies from New York musical theatre enjoyed artistic and commercial successes on the Great White Way. *Cabin* opened between two Ethel Merman hits, created for her by Cole Porter: *DuBarry Was a Lady* (46th Street Theatre, December 6, 1939) and *Panama Hattie* (46th Street Theatre, October 30, 1940). Vivienne Segal headlined in Rodgers and Hart's *Pal Joey* (Ethel Barrymore Theatre, December 25, 1940), and Gertrude Lawrence starred in Kurt Weill and Ira Gershwin's *Lady in the Dark* (Alvin Theatre, January 23, 1941). With *Cabin*, Ethel took her place with these great Broadway stars in the first-ever Broadway "book" musical (as opposed to a musical revue) to headline a black actress. Previously, only Adelaide Hall, who costarred with Bill "Bojangles" Robinson in *Brown Buddies* (1930), had headlined in a book musical on Broadway. But with *Cabin*, Ethel received solo billing above the title, the first time a black actress had been so honored in a musical production. *Cabin* was also the first major musical to be staged at the Martin Beck Theatre (on 45th Street, west of 8th Avenue).

Written by Lynn Root, with music by Vernon Duke and lyrics by John La-Touche, *Cabin* was a parable of faith, temptation, loyalty, and salvation in a black community in the Deep South. Petunia Jackson (Ethel Waters), a God-fearing, domesticated housewife, tries to keep her good-hearted but weak-willed husband Little Joe (Dooley Wilson) on the straight and narrow, but Lucifer Junior (Rex Ingram) is determined to make Little Joe backslide—and take Petunia with him. Lucifer Junior's plan involves a beautiful temptress (Katherine Dunham), who attempts to woo Little Joe away from his home-loving wife and lead him into trouble.

Cabin was directed and choreographed by the innovative George Balanchine, who later recalled how the show was cast after Ethel had been approached: "We wanted to have Cab Calloway in this play. He used to be singing, you know, jive. We wanted him as the devil, but we couldn't get him—he was too rich at that time. We wanted Rochester [as Little Joe], and Rochester wanted to do it but Ethel Waters didn't want him. So then we found this Dooley Wilson. . . . I thought it was very nice."[1]

At first, Ethel rejected the role of the devout Petunia, who makes a deal with God to save her good-for-nothing husband, Little Joe, who has been fatally injured in a street fight. She felt Lynn Root's libretto favored Little Joe and that Petunia, in the original script, was no more than a punching bag for her husband. Ethel also objected to the way religion was being handled. After changes were made, Ethel signed a contract, but in rehearsals, and even after the show had opened, she kept adding her own lines and "bits of business" to build up the character of Petunia. According to Allen Woll, "Waters changed the character to a woman of inner strength. Waters explained the transformation in a 1940 interview when she noted that the producers realized that she was the only one 'who could speak to the God [she] reveres without being ridiculed.' Petunia's steadfast faith was a strong and somewhat unexpected center for the show. And the role furthered Waters' growing reputation as a dramatic actress."[2] It worked, because Ethel's performance in *Cabin* received rave reviews, and it is generally acknowledged to be her finest on Broadway. She was applauded from all sides, especially for her renderings of such great songs as "Cabin in the Sky," "Honey in the Honeycomb," and, especially, the joyous "Taking a Chance on Love" (lyrics cowritten with Ted Fetter), which brought the house down every night. Theatre critic Brooks Atkinson comments in the *New York Times* (November 3, 1940): "Ethel Waters has never given a performance as rich as this before. This theatregoer imagines that he has never heard a song better sung than 'Taking a Chance on Love.' She stood that song on its head and ought to receive a Congressional Medal by way of award."

Ethel was the star of *Cabin*, but featured player Katherine Dunham, the celebrated dancer, choreographer, and anthropologist, who triumphantly pioneered musical revues on black themes, was also singled out by reviewers for special praise. Backstage, there was tension, as described by Dunham's biographer, Joyce Aschenbrenner:

> Waters, unlike Dunham, was not diplomatic in her professional relations. There were problems over dressing room assignments. Waters objected to be-

ing placed next to the bathroom, though it was intended as a convenience: "I told them they better not put me next to these shit houses." According to Dunham, Waters was a "great, great woman" who had "black anger" against whites. . . . Waters brushed off Dunham's background with "I don't know nothin' about no anthropology, but I do know about wigglin' your behind." She was suspicious of Dunham's support of unions, because the crews she had toured with were non-union. Moreover, she refused to join the fight for hotel rooms, since she preferred to stay with acquaintances in black neighbourhoods. It was a classic conflict of class and regional backgrounds.[3]

Dunham admired Ethel, but the star of *Cabin* proved to be a problem to the younger woman, who was struggling to hold her own in musical comedy, a field she knew nothing about, which included not only dancing but acting and singing as well. Dunham later reveals her feelings about Ethel and their troubled relationship:

> I didn't feel I was willing to be overshadowed simply because she was the star of the show. Ethel Waters was a difficult person, and I think it was because of her experience in an all-white Broadway theater. She's one of the greatest actresses I've known, and I still don't think she ever came into her own or did what she should have done. I would like to have seen her doing serious dramatic roles like Lady Macbeth, but because she was black she didn't. I think she knew this and it made her feel frustrated, so at times she showed these frustrations through her nervous tension. I realize now that anyone with a star's responsibility operates under this kind of tension that sometimes appears to be jealousy or what we think of as a "difficult character." I would say that Ethel Waters did exhibit a certain amount of jealousy—not just toward me, but toward the whole company. When you're starring and some other person or group of persons can get just as much applause as you do at a certain time, I think everyone has a certain jealous feeling. I know I would. This is the way I felt when Avon Long stole the show in *Carib Song* [1945], but it didn't keep me from realizing that I had learned a great deal from Ethel Waters. The natural jealousy of star to a rising star was there in *Cabin in the Sky*.[4]

Vernon Duke had been forewarned about Ethel's temperament and understood that she had a reputation for being an extremely difficult woman to work with, "but I won her over by a time-honored device. . . . I kissed her hand in lieu of 'Good morning' and 'Be seeing you.'" Duke introduced her in his book *Passport to Paris* as "that wonderful woman."[5] Henry Pleasants explains in *The Great American Popular Singers* that "a certain old-worldliness in Duke (he was Russian) may have rendered him more aware of, and more sympathetic to, the sense of personal dignity, even of rank, characteristic of the older black artists." Duke was, Pleasants says, spared the lesson learned by John La-

Touche after the first-night audience responded so positively and enthusiastically to Ethel's rendition of "Taking a Chance on Love": "He rushed back stage to her dressing room to congratulate her, crying 'Ethel!' . . . She just sat there, looked up at him, and said, 'Miss Waters.'"[6]

Cabin closed on March 8, 1941, after 156 performances. The show had established Ethel as one of the great names in Broadway musical "book" theatre. She had reached the top of her profession and was considered one of the most famous—and celebrated—African American stars of her generation. She took her place alongside such names as Louis Armstrong, Marian Anderson, Duke Ellington, and Paul Robeson, but there was one medium she had yet to conquer: cinema. With Cabin, it was only a matter of time before Hollywood beckoned. An opportunity for Ethel came when producer Arthur Freed, who worked at MGM and had recently scored a hit with The Wizard of Oz, starring Judy Garland, purchased the screen rights for Cabin.

Ethel's previous film appearances had been limited to a handful of guest roles and leads in short subjects. A screen version of Cabin would enable Ethel to establish herself in the medium as a leading lady, almost unprecedented in Hollywood for a black actress. Until the early 1940s, only Nina Mae McKinney in MGM's Hallelujah! (1929) had played a starring role. In the 1930s, Ethel's contemporaries found starring roles in European movies: Josephine Baker in France, in Zou Zou (1934) and Princess Tam Tam (1935); and Elisabeth Welch as Paul Robeson's leading lady in two British films, Song of Freedom (1936) and Big Fella (1937). There were leading roles for black actresses such as Ethel Moses, Evelyn Preer, Edna Mae Harris, and Francine Everett in American "race" movies, produced independently, outside Hollywood, but these reached limited audiences. The movie capital of the world cold-shouldered black leading ladies, but this changed when Ethel was invited to repeat her Cabin role on film.

At first, MGM's announcement that they would be making a film version of Cabin was met with disapproval from all sides. White studio executives were apprehensive, fearing such a venture would not make money, and the black press was concerned that the film would perpetuate racial stereotypes. In press interviews, Freed tried to allay such fears: "I will spare nothing and will put everything behind it. It will be a picture on a par with any major film under the MGM banner."[7] On Cabin, Freed gave the Broadway director Vincente Minnelli his first feature assignment. Minnelli had a reputation for taste and style, and he had already worked with Ethel on At Home Abroad. Minnelli planned to approach the subject "with great affection rather than condescension. . . . A portion of the militant black and liberal white press was highly critical of the proposed endeavour, finding the story patronizing.

But there were an equal number of publications supporting us. . . . We would never knowingly affront blacks. . . . or anyone else for that matter."[8] Filming commenced on *Cabin* in August 1942, with only Ethel and Rex Ingram being retained from the Broadway cast. Eddie "Rochester" Anderson replaced Dooley Wilson. At that time, cinema audiences were more familiar with Rochester, who had been working in Hollywood since the early 1930s and was best known for playing Jack Benny's valet in comedy films. Wilson would eventually make his mark in Hollywood in 1943 as Sam, Humphrey Bogart's piano-playing sidekick, in *Casablanca*. The character of Georgia Brown, instead of being the dancing part that Katherine Dunham had played on Broadway, was revised as a singing role tailor-made for Lena Horne. Extra added attractions included jazz giants Louis Armstrong and Duke Ellington, dance innovator John "Bubbles" Sublett, Butterfly McQueen (from *Gone with the Wind*), and the Hall Johnson Choir.

During preproduction, it was decided to interpolate additional songs to enhance the plot. However, the original composers were not available. Consequently, Harold Arlen and E. Y. "Yip" Harburg were engaged to write some new songs, including one for Ethel to sing while Little Joe is convalescing. The result was "Happiness Is a Thing Called Joe," and it proved to be a resounding success, earning the film's only Oscar nomination, in the best song category. It lost out to Harry Warren and Mack David's sentimental wartime favorite "You'll Never Know," sung by Alice Faye in Fox's *Hello, Frisco, Hello.*

In 1942 Lena Horne signed a seven-year contract with MGM and was looking forward to working with her close friend Vincente Minnelli. However, as she explains in her autobiography *Lena* (1966), she had been warned that Ethel could be temperamental and tough on other singers. Ethel, fearing that MGM would promote Lena at her expense, stipulated in her contract (worth $25,000) that, in the screen credits, no member of the cast was to appear in type larger than that used to portray her name.

Lena acknowledged that Ethel had been "terribly exploited" and had become suspicious of everyone connected to the film, especially the studio bosses, but nothing could have prepared her for Ethel's outburst on the set of *Cabin*. Lena had been enjoying herself but was aware that Ethel resented her being cast in the film: "She thought others deserved the part more and that I was part of the plot against her that she was sure the studio bosses had concocted. . . . With all this tension building up, I was prepared to be very, very careful when we finally started working together."[9]

When film historian Edward Mapp was growing up in Harlem in the 1930s and 1940s, he heard people talk about Ethel and realized she was an icon, but it didn't mean anything to him. The first time she became part of his direct experience was when he saw the film version of *Cabin*, which he loved:

> I particularly enjoyed Ethel singing "Taking a Chance on Love." She sang it beautifully. Ethel had worked hard for years and paid her dues. *Cabin* was to be her film, the one that would put her on the map in Hollywood. But MGM had just signed the young and beautiful Lena Horne to a seven year contract and the studio planned to co-star her with Ethel in *Cabin*. Ethel was middle-aged, and did not have youth and beauty on her side, or the security of a long-term contract. For Ethel, this was a one-picture deal. So naturally she felt threatened by the presence of Lena in her film. I don't think she meant to be mean to Lena. I really don't. But Ethel must have been upset about Lena attracting attention.[10]

Ethel's first show of anger occurred in the sound department. According to Lena's daughter, Gail Lumet Buckley, "When Ethel heard Lena's recording of 'Honey in the Honeycomb,' she accused Lena of parodying her singing style. By now Lena was getting a bit nervous. It was almost time for her to shoot her scene with Ethel."[11] Lena believed filming might have progressed smoothly if it hadn't been for an accident that occurred the day before her scene with Ethel was due to be filmed. While rehearsing a dance number, Lena fell and hurt her ankle: "Rochester swore that he had seen Ethel making voodoo signs over the spot where Lena fell. Lena only half laughed."[12] The following day, Lena received a great deal of attention while, in an attempt to hide the fact that her ankle was in plaster, the dance was restaged and difficult camera angles were altered. "The atmosphere was very tense and it exploded when a prop man brought a pillow for me to put under my sore ankle. Miss Waters started to blow like a hurricane. It was an all-encompassing blow, touching everyone and everything that got in its way. Though I (or my ankle) may have been the immediate cause of it, it was actually directed at everything that had made her life miserable, the whole system that had held her back and exploited her."[13] As Duke Ellington might have put it, "My dear, she wrote the history of jazz." Gail Lumet Buckley comments: "You could hear a pin drop. Everyone stood rooted in silence while Ethel's eruption shook the sound stage. She went on and on. Arthur Freed and Ethel's agent appeared on the set. She was still more or less raving when Vincente dismissed the company and suspended shooting for the day. Lena was shaking. . . . All the black actors eyed one another nervously and spoke among themselves in whispers. The next day, however, the scene was rehearsed and shot impeccably. . . . Lena and Ethel never spoke again."[14]

Gail claims that Ethel's diatribe began with attacks on Lena and ended with a vilification of Hollywood Jews and that it was her vocal anti-Semitism that made her unemployable in Hollywood for six years. However, Edward Mapp offers a different interpretation of Ethel's outburst:

> I have not heard these allegations of anti-Semitism. I would say that it was more anti-power structure. If you're having a hard time, and you're a powerless black woman, even though you're famous, I think you will lash out at the people who are exploiting you. It just happened that these were white people, there were no black studio heads in Hollywood and the vast majority of studio heads were not only white, but Jewish. People love to put a spin on things and I bet they said, "Oh, Ethel is anti-Semitic," but I don't think so. Her anger was directed at who she felt was exploiting her. There's an expression, "Please get your foot off my neck." These things have a way of taking off. Chinese whispers. It started as one story and ended up as another. And I think that's what happened to Ethel and her so-called anti-Semitic outburst. I just don't think there was something in her nature to be that way. She might have been a lot of other things, but I don't think that! One of the most moving moments I've ever experienced was an Ethel Waters moment. When she sings "Supper Time." When she finishes that, you just want to start crying. It's just so moving because the story was a comment on racism in the United States. She's preparing the evening meal, and the kids are there in the kitchen, but the husband doesn't come home because he's been lynched. And this was written by Irving Berlin, who'd written more light-hearted songs like "Easter Parade." He was Jewish. So was Harold Arlen who composed the music for "Stormy Weather," and whom Ethel affectionately described as "the Negro-ist white man" she had ever known. Ethel included the Yiddish "Eli, Eli" as part of her cabaret repertoire. So how can we reconcile that with Ethel being anti-Semitic?[15]

When *Cabin* was released it was Lena, not Ethel, whom MGM sent to New York to promote the film with Duke Ellington's band when they showcased it at the Capitol Theatre. MGM always sent their contract players out to promote their films with personal appearances. The studio promoted Lena as the star of the film, not Ethel. All through the production of *Cabin*, Ethel must have felt threatened, very insecure, hurt, and maybe even jealous. It was a terrible situation for her. Understandably, Ethel barely mentions *Cabin* in her 1951 autobiography, other than to comment that "there was conflict between the studio and me from the beginning . . . all through that picture there was so much snarling and scrapping that I don't know how in the world *Cabin in the Sky* ever stayed up there. I won all my battles on that picture. But like many other performers, I was to discover that winning arguments in Hollywood is costly. Six years were to pass before I could get another movie job."[16]

The main beneficiaries of *Cabin's* success were Lena, who went on to make another black-cast musical success, *Stormy Weather*, for 20th Century Fox, as well as many guest appearances in popular MGM musical extravaganzas, and Vincente Minnelli. He went on to make a succession of wonderful films for MGM, including such musical classics as *Meet Me in St. Louis* (1944), *An American in Paris* (1951), and *Gigi* (1958), for which he received an Oscar for best director. In a long film career, Minnelli worked with such famous leading ladies as Judy Garland, Katharine Hepburn, Elizabeth Taylor, Lana Turner, Lucille Ball, Judy Holliday, Barbra Streisand, Ingrid Bergman, and daughter Liza. In his autobiography, he remembers Ethel's performance in his first directorial assignment. For him, Ethel successfully "translated her bravura, outsize stage performance into a more naturalistic film portrayal. She owed it to her very expressive face and eyes."[17]

Minnelli could, and should, have said more about Ethel, for she is the heart and soul of *Cabin*, his first movie. Her performance is one of the best in the Hollywood musical genre, ranking alongside Judy Garland in *A Star Is Born*, Doris Day in *The Pajama Game*, Julie Andrews in *The Sound of Music*, and Barbra Streisand in *Funny Girl*. The film includes a rich array of musical highlights, and some of the best feature Ethel. She gives terrific interpretations of "Happiness Is a Thing Called Joe" and "Taking a Chance on Love." The latter was included in MGM's compilation feature *That's Entertainment! Part 2* (1976). When Petunia pursues her estranged husband to the nightclub, she transforms herself from a God-fearing housewife into a glamorous diva in an attempt to win back her man from the temptress Georgia Brown. In the wonderful nightclub sequence, which features the glorious music of Duke Ellington and his band, Ethel reprises Lena's song "Honey in the Honeycomb" in a dazzling production number. Halfway through the number she unexpectedly launches into a lively jitterbug, which she performs effortlessly with the great John "Bubbles" Sublett. It is an unforgettable moment in the history of movie musicals.

Ethel should have been nominated for an Oscar in one of the most uninspiring years for best actress nominees. In the 1943 lineup were the winner, Jennifer Jones (*The Song of Bernadette*), and nominees Jean Arthur (*The More the Merrier*), Ingrid Bergman (*For Whom the Bell Tolls*), Joan Fontaine (*The Constant Nymph*), and Greer Garson (*Madame Curie*). But there were two factors against Ethel. First, she was black. Not until 1954 would a black actress be nominated in the leading category, when Dorothy Dandridge was recognized for *Carmen Jones*. Second, the American Academy of Motion

Picture Arts and Sciences has been very poor at recognizing musical and comedy performances. Very few have been nominated since the first awards were presented in 1927–1928. Even Danny Peary in his book *Alternate Oscars* (1993), in which he second-guessed the Academy Awards in every year, overlooked Ethel, as he did her 1952 appearance in *The Member of the Wedding*.

Ethel's performance in *Cabin* has stood the test of time and always draws praise from critics and film historians. In 1967 Douglas McVay wrote in *The Musical Film* that "the angels also have on their side the inestimable advantage of Ethel Waters, who never puts a foot wrong—whether informing us that 'Happiness is a Thing Called Joe,' or 'Taking a Chance on Love' in a way that transforms a commercial number into a rich expression of *bienetre*, or mocking the sultry siren (Lena Horne) with her own bounteous interpretation of 'Honey in the Honeycomb,' or merely dreaming of that cabin in the sky."[18] In 1981 Clive Hirschhorn wrote the following: "The undoubted star of *Cabin in the Sky* is the inimitable Ethel Waters, about whom a New York magazine at the time bluntly declared: 'If it wasn't for her colour, Miss Waters would undoubtedly become one of Hollywood's top names.' Her performance is superb, and her singing of 'Happiness is a Thing Called Joe' a highlight in a film which, though manacled by the kind of cosy stereotyping so deplored by black audiences, is nonetheless full of magical musical moments."[19] In 1982 Ethan Mordden observed in *The Hollywood Musical* that "Waters takes the screen and holds it; the prize number consists of Waters just standing there, handkerchief in hand, singing 'Taking a Chance on Love.'"[20] In his Hall of Fame and Disrepute, Mordden selects Ethel in *Cabin* as one of the best performances in a Hollywood musical in an eclectic list that features eighteen other artists from 1929 to 1979, including Helen Morgan (*Show Boat*), Bert Lahr (*The Wizard of Oz*), Judy Garland (*The Wizard of Oz* and *A Star Is Born*), James Cagney (*Yankee Doodle Dandy*), Rita Moreno (*West Side Story*), Barbra Streisand (*Funny Girl*), Nipsey Russell (*The Wiz*), and Bette Midler (*The Rose*). Mordden also includes Ethel's performance of "Taking a Chance on Love" in his list of best musical numbers. Perhaps the final word should go to Geoff Andrew, who summed up the appeal of *Cabin* when he wrote the following in the London listings magazine *Time Out*: "One can easily criticise this all-black musical for falling prey to 'Uncle Tom' stereotyping but there's no denying both the compassion with which Minnelli treats his characters and the immense cinematic talent on view. . . . the cast are magnificent, delivering the lovely score with style and power."[21]

Notes

1. George Balanchine, *On Broadway* (London: Thames and Hudson, 1979), 14.

2. Allen Woll, *Black Musical Theatre: From Coontown to Dreamgirls* (Baton Rouge: Louisiana State University Press, 1989), 195.

3. Joyce Aschenbrenner, *Katherine Dunham: Dancing a Life* (Urbana: University of Illinois Press, 2002), 167–68.

4. Ruth Beckford, *Katherine Dunham: A Biography* (New York: Dekker, 1979), 105–6.

5. Henry Pleasants, *The Great American Popular Singers* (London: Gollancz, 1974), 90.

6. Pleasants, *Popular Singers*, 90.

7. Hugh Fordin, *The World of Entertainment! Hollywood's Greatest Musicals* (New York: Doubleday, 1975), 71.

8. Vincente Minnelli with Hector Arce, *I Remember It Well* (London: Angus and Robertson, 1975), 121.

9. Lena Horne with Richard Schickel, *Lena* (London: Deutsch, 1966), 152.

10. Edward Mapp, interview with Stephen Bourne, London, August 15, 2005.

11. Gail Lumet Buckley, *The Hornes: An American Family* (London: Weidenfeld and Nicholson, 1987), 164.

12. Lumet Buckley, *The Hornes*, 165.

13. Horne, *Lena*, 154.

14. Lumet Buckley, *The Hornes*, 165.

15. Mapp interview

16. Ethel Waters with Charles Samuels, *His Eye Is on the Sparrow* (New York: Da Capo, 1992), 258.

17. Minnelli, *I Remember*, 126.

18. Douglas McVay, *The Musical Film* (London: Zwemmer, 1967), 42–43.

19. Clive Hirschhorn, "In the Picture," *Radio Times*, October 10–16, 1981.

20. Ethan Mordden, *The Hollywood Musical* (Newton Abbot, U.K.: David and Charles, 1982), 177.

21. Geoff Andrew, *Time Out Film Guide*, 9th ed., ed. John Pym (London: Penguin, 2001), 159.

Ethel as a child

Ethel in drag in the 1920s

Supper Time (As Thousands Cheer, *1933)*

Heat Wave (As Thousands Cheer, *1933)*

At Home Abroad *(1935)*

Ethel in the 1930s

Mamba's Daughters *(1939)*

Ethel (1943)

Ethel, Kenneth Spencer, Eddie Anderson, Lena Horne, and Rex Ingram in Cabin in the Sky *(1943)*

Ethel and John W. Sublett in Cabin in the Sky *(1943)*

Ethel as Petunia in Cabin in the Sky, *by Albert Leonard*

Ethel and Jeanne Crain in Pinky *(1949)*

Brandon de Wilde, Ethel, and Julie Harris in The Member of the Wedding *(1952)*

Ethel at a Billy Graham concert event in the 1970s, by Albert Leonard

CHAPTER SEVEN

~

Hollywood

Prior to filming *Cabin*, Ethel had already filmed two Hollywood productions, both released in August 1942, just a week or so before filming commenced on *Cabin*. In a segment of 20th Century Fox's *Tales of Manhattan* (1942), directed by Julian Duvivier, she starred opposite Paul Robeson as a sharecropper's wife, and in MGM's *Cairo* (1942), directed by W. S. Van Dyke, she played Jeanette MacDonald's maid.

Tales of Manhattan marked Paul Robeson's return to Hollywood for the first time since Universal's *Show Boat* (1936), but it proved to be an unhappy experience for him. In the 1930s he had established himself as a major screen personality in Britain, but he probably suffered more disappointments than any other film actor of his generation. Black characters in American films of the period rarely moved beyond Al Jolson in blackface, or dim-witted buffoons played by African Americans such as Stepin Fetchit and Willie "Sleep 'n' Eat" Best. For an intelligent and progressive actor such as Robeson, there were hardly any opportunities to play challenging roles, though he did establish himself in British cinema as a popular leading man in productions such as *Song of Freedom* (1936), *Jericho* (1937), *Big Fella* (1937), and *The Proud Valley* (1940) before returning to America at the outbreak of war in Europe in September 1939.

Robeson's decision to return to Hollywood to play the sharecropper in *Tales of Manhattan* was not taken lightly, but it proved to be one he deeply regretted making. The film consisted of six stories connected through the travels of a dress coat as it passes from owner to owner, and each episode featured some of the biggest names then working in Hollywood: Charles Boyer, Rita Hayworth, Ginger Rogers, Henry Fonda, Charles Laughton, and Edward G. Robinson. In the final segment, the coat, with a stolen $43,000 in the pocket, falls from a plane onto a plot of land farmed by poor black sharecroppers: Luke (Paul Robeson) and his wife Esther (Ethel Waters). They take the money to Reverend Lazarus (Eddie "Rochester" Anderson), who makes the ridiculous claim that it is "more money than there is in the whole world!" He divides the money among the inhabitants of the community, which is regrettably full of Hollywood stereotypes: quaint, God-fearing, superstitious, Hallelujah-shouting "colored" folk. These include Grandpa (Clarence Muse), who asks the Reverend for $25 for a coffin to take him through the "pearly gates" of Heaven.

Surprisingly Robeson doesn't help matters. His portrayal of Luke is embarrassing. There is no hint of the "natural" acting style he brought to some of his earlier British films, notably *Song of Freedom* and *The Proud Valley*. His shuffling, awkward posturing is uncomfortably close to Stepin Fetchit. In this film, Robeson is not in the same league as his costars, Ethel and Rochester, who have had more experience at playing this kind of American vision of black folk. They play the Hollywood game and turn their stereotypical characters on their heads. Robeson doesn't. He's lost.

Toward the end of the story, Robeson shares a brief but memorable scene with veteran Hollywood actor George Reed (1866–1952), who began his film career in the silent era and earned more than one hundred credits, mostly as railroad porters and servants. At the climax of the segment, Robeson sings "Glory Day" with the Hall Johnson Choir, his hands raised to heaven.

Robeson's biographer, Martin Bauml Duberman, believed that the appeal to Robeson "lay in a chance to depict the plight of the rural black poor, shown in the film, as investing the bulk of their windfall in communal land and tools," adding that "some black reviewers, focusing on the film's depiction of sharecropping, came out in its favour. But the majority did not, with the New York *Amsterdam Star News* headlining in its negative review 'Paul Robeson, Ethel Waters Let Us Down.'"[1]

Most reviews from white critics were favorable, though Bosley Crowther in the *New York Times* (September 25, 1942) mentions the final segment only in passing and ignores Robeson altogether. Archer Winsten criticizes the black characters in the *New York Post* (September 25, 1942): "These Negroes are ignorant, child-like, tuneful creatures." Black reviewers were unhappy, especially with Robeson. The *Amsterdam New York Star News* (August 15, 1942) asks, "Why must our greatest stars of music and stage be forever relegated to humiliating roles?" and the left-wing, white-run African American *PM* (September 25, 1942) comments that other members of the black press objected to the black characters being associated with "superstition, childishness and placed in an unreal setting." However, Walter White of the NAACP (National Association for the Advancement of Colored People) is quoted in the same issue of *PM* as saying that, on the whole, the setting was real in that it depicted the true economic status of blacks and showed the black characters not in a servile or clownish position, and that the dreams, prayers, and desires of the people were for real things. It was also reported (in *PM*, September 22, 1942) that Southern distributors and exhibitors attacked the film because it ended with a sequence featuring black actors and Robeson's uttering of "communistic" sentiments. After the film's release, Robeson was condemned for perpetuating a Hollywood racial stereotype. He agreed with his critics, publicly stating in *PM* (September 22, 1942) that he "wouldn't blame any Negro for picketing the film. . . . when I first read the script I told them it was silly," but he had hoped he could change it during the filming. Two days later, the following appeared in the *New York Times* (September 24, 1942):

> Paul Robeson said today he was through with Hollywood until movie magnates found some other way to portray the Negro besides the usual "plantation hallelujah shouters." In an interview the Negro baritone said he was particularly despondent over his recent return to Hollywood to play a sharecropper sequence in *Tales of Manhattan*. "I thought I could change the picture as we went along," Robeson said, "and I did make some headway. But in the end it turned out to be the same old thing—the Negro solving his problem by singing his way to glory. This is very offensive to my people. It makes the Negro child-like and innocent and is in the old plantation tradition. But Hollywood says you can't make the Negro in any other role because it won't be box office in the South. The South wants its Negroes in the old style."

When *Tales of Manhattan* opened in Los Angeles, the militant newspaper *Sentinel and Tribune* organized pickets to demonstrate. Robeson then volunteered to join protestors outside cinemas where the film was being shown. In interviews, he explained how he had been led to believe he would be able to make script changes, but these were rejected. He never made another film as an actor. Years later, film historian Thomas Cripps describes the dilemma Robeson faced in Hollywood in 1942: "Robeson, despondent and bitter, told an interviewer that his film career was at an end. . . . Forced to choose between long-standing loyalty to cinema and his faith in the politics of the left, he chose the latter and blasted the picture he had liked enough to appear in and fight to change."[2]

In her autobiography, Ethel notes the amount of money she had been offered to portray Esther: $10,000 ($1,000 a day for ten days' work); expresses her disappointment with the cutting of a sequence in which she sang "Nobody Knows the Trouble I've Seen"; and comments that, when the film was released, "various Negro organizations picketed the theatres showing it. Their placards protested picturing us colored people as wretched, dirty, and poorly clad. I didn't understand that. These same organizations were forever complaining that we Negroes in America are underprivileged. So why did they object to anyone showing us that way on the screen? . . . Why some of us should want Negroes to be portrayed as neat, clean Elsie Dinsmores and Little Lord Fauntleroys baffles me. Those are white characters, brother, and damn bores. I'm for letting the white folks keep them for themselves."[3]

Film historian David Shipman describes the Robeson and Waters segment as "folksy and patronizing . . . a negation of everything both artists stood for,"[4] while celebrated African American author James Baldwin, in *The Devil Finds Work* (1976), his superb study of Hollywood cinema, makes the following observation:

> It is scarcely possible to think of a black American actor who has not been misused: not one has ever been seriously challenged to deliver the best that is in him. The most powerful examples of this cowardice and waste are the careers of Paul Robeson and Ethel Waters. If they had ever been allowed really to hit their stride, they might immeasurably have raised the level of cinema and theater in this country. . . . It is pointless, however, to pursue this, and personally painful: Mr Robeson is declining, in obscurity, and Miss Waters is singing in Billy Graham's choir. They might have been treated with more respect by the country to which they gave so much. What the black actor has managed to give are moments—indelible moments, created, miraculously, beyond the confines of the script; hints of reality, smuggled like contraband into a maudlin tale, and with enough force, if unleashed, to shatter the tale to fragments.[5]

Baldwin then lists some of the black actors who, in his opinion, had given such "moments" in Hollywood cinema: Sidney Poitier (*The Defiant Ones*), Juano Hernandez (*Young Man with a Horn, Intruder in the Dust*), Canada Lee (*Body and Soul*), Rochester (*The Green Pastures, Tales of Manhattan*), Paul Robeson ("in everything I saw him do"), and Ethel Waters in *The Member of the Wedding* (see chapter 9).

Not long after Lena Horne signed her contract with MGM, she was screen-tested for the role of a maid, Cleona Jones, in *Cairo*, a spoof on spy thrillers, starring Jeanette MacDonald and Robert Young. When Lena negotiated the contract with MGM, her father insisted that the studio not cast her as a maid. However, in her autobiography, Lena acknowledges that the maid in *Cairo* "was a good role—the maid was to be just as flippant and fresh as anyone. She was a human being, not a stereotype." Lena made the screen test with Eddie "Rochester" Anderson, but she described it as a "farce": "They wanted me to match Rochester's color so they kept smearing dark make-up on me. . . . the test was a disaster. I looked as if I were some white person trying to do a part in blackface. I did not do the picture; Ethel Waters got the part."[6]

Opera diva Jeanette MacDonald had enjoyed nine years of stardom as one of MGM's most popular leading ladies. She was also one of the favorites of studio head Louis B. Mayer. *Cairo* marked the end of her MGM reign, and it was her least successful film for the studio, both artistically and financially. John McClain's script (from an "idea" by Ladislaus Fodor) is confusing and undistinguished. However, one of the strengths of *Cairo* is that, throughout the film, Jeanette and her costar Ethel enjoy a friendly, relaxed relationship. The actresses seem to be enjoying each other's company. Though Ethel wears a maid's uniform, she behaves more like a companion than a servant to Jeanette, and their on-screen partnership has a warmth that is lacking in most Hollywood depictions of white mistress–black maid relationships. Cleona Jones is, indeed, as "flippant and fresh" as Lena Horne discovered when she made the screen test, and Ethel plays her with a sense of fun. For example, when Robert Young, employed as Jeanette's butler, fails to answer the telephone, Ethel breezes past him and quips, "The reason a phone rings is so that a butler knows when to answer it!" Earlier she complains to Jeanette about being away from America for too long (the film is set in Libya and in the city of Cairo): "I've been away as long as you have Miss Marcia. I miss everything you miss plus a nice colored boy who speaks something besides French or goes around in a nightgown in which case he turns out to be a Arab."

Ethel participated in several musical sequences. First there is a duet between Jeanette and Ethel, which takes place with Jeanette in the bath and Ethel bustling about the bedroom. The duet includes fragments from Luigi Arditi's "Il Bacio" and Donizetti's "Sextet from *Lucia di Lammermoor*" as well as a sort-of operatic recitative about the whereabouts of towels and the like. Real weird! Later, at a rehearsal at Marcia Warren's home with a male vocal quartet and some musicians, a lengthy medley contrasts Jeanette's "high brow" opera singing with Ethel's "Harlemesque" take on the old favorite "Waiting for the Robert E. Lee" (also known as "See Them Shufflin' Along"). Ethel's brief but lively rendition is followed by a reprise of the same number by Jeanette, which is highly embarrassing.

Ethel has only one big number in the film, but it is a decent one. "Buds Won't Bud," with music by Harold Arlen and lyrics by E. Y. "Yip" Harburg, had been written for their 1937 stage musical *Hooray for What!* The song was introduced by Hannah Williams in the pre-Broadway tryout but cut from the show before it reached Broadway. After the show closed, MGM bought the rights but never filmed it. Instead they used its songs in other films including *Babes in Arms* (1939), starring Judy Garland and Mickey Rooney. It was Garland who was first scheduled to sing "Buds Won't Bud" in a movie, *Andy Hardy Meets Debutante* (1940), but the song was cut. Eventually it found its way into *Cairo*, and Ethel's spirited rendition of the swing number is one of the film's highlights.

Following this number, Dooley Wilson, Ethel's costar from the Broadway version of *Cabin*, makes a welcome appearance as Hector in the role originally intended for Rochester. Hector explains he has been living in the desert for four years. Back home in America "there wasn't a Arab picture shooting that I didn't play a Arab. The only time I was eating was when I was being a Arab. So I said to myself, maybe you're a Arab at heart and you just won't give in. So I gave in. I beat my way over here, and here I am." Romance blossoms between Cleona and Hector when they perform a lovely reprise of "Buds Won't Bud." The following year, Dooley gained screen immortality as Sam, the piano player who sings "As Time Goes By," in the Warner Bros. classic *Casablanca*.

In *The Films of Jeanette MacDonald and Nelson Eddy* (1975), Eleanor Knowles writes: "Ethel Waters was a box-office question mark, and promotion for *Cairo* carefully captioned her picture 'Broadway Musical Comedy Star.' Black performers were still either servants or nightclub performers who could be easily snipped out of prints for Southern distribution. . . . With her zest, sparkling good humour, and ultimate dignity, she comes close to stealing *Cairo* from its nominal stars, despite her brief footage."[7]

During the war, several Hollywood studios produced all-star musical extravaganzas featuring their contract players, who provided songs, dances, and comedy sketches. The novelty of seeing a great dramatic star such as Bette Davis sing and jitterbug proved to be popular with wartime audiences and servicemen. Most of these films, which include Paramount's *Star Spangled Rhythm* (1942), MGM's *Thousands Cheer* (1943), and Warner Bros.' *Thank Your Lucky Stars* (1943), featured musical sequences for black artistes. For example, Rochester and Katherine Dunham perform "Smart as a Tack" in *Star Spangled Rhythm*, Lena Horne sings "Honeysuckle Rose" in *Thousands Cheer*, and Hattie McDaniel livens up *Thank Your Lucky Stars* with "Ice Cold Katie." United Artists' *Stage Door Canteen* (1943), directed by Frank Borzage and released shortly after *Cabin*, featured Ethel with Count Basie and His Orchestra. She sang Al Dubin and James V. Monaco's "Quicksand," specially written for the film. Other musical interludes were provided by Britain's Gracie Fields, an up-and-coming Peggy Lee (with Benny Goodman and His Orchestra), and Ethel Merman.

Because it was difficult to film at the actual Stage Door Canteen on 44th Street in New York, it was duplicated at two filming locations: Fox News N.Y. Studios and RKO-Pathe Studios in Culver City. Its all-star cast also featured a host of other top names (mostly leading ladies) from the world of theatre. The film was basically a tribute to the American Theatre Wing, who sponsored the movie and offered audiences a glimpse of the sort of entertainment servicemen might, if they were lucky, expect to see on any given night of the week at the celebrated Stage Door Canteen. In addition to Ethel, the stars on parade included Tallulah Bankhead, Katharine Cornell, Lynn Fontanne, Helen Hayes, Katharine Hepburn, and Gertrude Lawrence. Even Gypsy Rose Lee got in on the act, though she didn't strip!

Stage Door Canteen was an uneven, overlong, and only occasionally entertaining extravaganza, but in spite of its flaws, it was one of the top moneymaking films of 1943, with 90 percent of the box-office takings going to the American Theatre Wing. However, for Ethel, the damage had been done. After her outburst on the set of *Cabin* (see chapter 6), her Hollywood career came to an abrupt end, just as it had peaked. However, a survey of roles for black actresses in Hollywood at that time reveals that, after *Cabin*, there was probably nowhere for Ethel to go anyway, with one possible exception.

Ethel might have been considered for an important role in the Warner Bros. melodrama *Saratoga Trunk*, filmed in 1943 but not released until the end of 1945. Ethel would have been ideal as Angelique Pluton, the French black servant of Clio Dulaine, a creole adventuress. The film was set in New Orleans in 1875. Ingrid Bergman was miscast as Clio, in a role that had probably been rejected by Bette Davis (then under contract to Warner Bros.) and certainly by Vivien Leigh. Either would have been more suitable in the role than Bergman. Regarding Ethel, presumably Warner Bros. felt the public would not take too well to a film in which an actual black woman exercised a powerful influence over the film's heroine, for Angelique is no mammy from *Gone with the Wind*. Overprotective of her mistress, she is a mysterious and sinister presence. The role went to the white British character actress Flora Robson, then working in Hollywood, who "blacked-up" for the part. However, Robson gave a memorable performance and earned an Oscar nomination for best supporting actress.

In 1981, Robson's biographer, Kenneth Barrow, claimed Flora was cast because Sam Wood, the film's director, hated black people: "And this was one
of the reasons for casting a white woman. Strangely, when Flora was made-
up, he treated her as though she really were black. Gone were all the niceties
he had used to charm her into accepting the role. For some of the scenes
Flora had to drive to different locations and was shocked to find exactly how
black people were treated. Policemen ordered her about and a crowd of sol-
diers shouted obscenities at her. She longed to pull back the collar of her
blouse and show she was white underneath."[8]

For Ethel, there was a return to Broadway in the variety revue *Laugh Time*,
which opened at the Shubert Theatre on September 8, 1943, and closed after
126 performances on November 20. Her costars included the great black song
and dance team Buck and Bubbles; Frank Fay, acknowledged as the first really
successful stand-up comedian and MC to work in nightclubs and in vaudeville; and comedian Bert Wheeler. Ethel explains in her autobiography that,
at this time, as far as her career was concerned, she was "sitting on top of the
world," but then it all began to fall apart. After *Laugh Time*, her professional
career came almost to a dead stop. She blamed agents, and it must have been
heartbreaking for the star who had worked so hard for success. After a long absence, another Broadway revue, *Blue Holiday*, was intended to be a vehicle for
Ethel's comeback. It opened at the Belasco Theatre on May 21, 1945, but
closed after eight performances, in spite of a stellar cast of black talent that included the Katherine Dunham Dancers, folk singer Josh White, singer and
dancer Josephine Premice (who, in the 1950s, would impress Broadway with
her featured roles in the musicals *House of Flowers* and *Jamaica*, for which she
was nominated for a Tony), and the great jazz pianist Mary Lou Williams.

With *Blue Holiday*, Ethel was anxious to reestablish herself as the Broadway star she had been five years earlier in *Cabin in the Sky*. The timing was
right. In the early 1940s there had been only a few decent opportunities for
black artistes on the Great White Way, but Broadway theatre was opening up
again for African Americans: Paul Robeson (*Othello*, 1943), Dooley Wilson
(*Bloomer Girl*, 1944), and Canada Lee (*The Tempest*, 1945) had all been acclaimed, but Ethel's "comeback" was doomed. She was panned by most of the
critics, and it must have been particularly galling when newcomer Josh
White received the best reviews for his performance of folk songs and contemporary numbers. According to Mary Lou Williams, "The whole thing was
kind of thrown together," and the cast treated Ethel as an "old has-been,"
laughing at her star airs.[9]

With *Blue Holiday*, Ethel had become the self-destructive star. She may
have blamed her agents for lack of work, but when something came her way,

though her intentions may have been for the good of the show, Ethel failed badly. Eartha Kitt, who was to become an international star in the 1950s, had only recently joined the Katherine Dunham company when she found herself in the cast of *Blue Holiday*:

> We girls were supposed to be Hawaiian dancers. We were dressed in very scanty costumes and then told to wiggle wiggle our way across the stage. Here we were all doing our wiggles when a voice screamed in the harshest tones, "Get those naked bitches off my stage!" This was the start of my experience in the theatre world. Thank God, this was only a rehearsal. We all looked in the direction from which the voice came, to be met by the thunderous sound of footsteps coming towards us from the wings. Ethel Waters came on stage with lightning speed, shooing us away with arms flailing. "I don't want those naked bitches on my stage. Get them damn things out of here!" she cried. She and the producers and directors had a small conference on stage as we hovered in the wings trying to hear what was being said. Eventually we were called back to begin our routine again on the beach-like stage. We continued to wiggle wiggle along when suddenly, without warning, a tap dancer (who turned out to be Ethel Waters' lover) entered on stage in front of us tapping on the beach in a routine from the Apollo Theatre. We all stood stunned, wondering how a tap dancer could tap on sand, but that was the way Ethel Waters wanted it and that was the way it stayed. Needless to say the show did not last.[10]

In 1947 there was talk of Ethel starring in a play called *I Talked with God*, a dramatization of the life of Sojourner Truth, who had been born into slavery and lived to become one of the greatest preachers of all time. Nothing came of the project. That same year, because of a mix-up, she narrowly missed returning to Broadway in an important dramatic role, the nurse in *Medea* with Judith Anderson and John Gielgud (who also directed). Ethel was heartbroken, revealing in her autobiography that she "sat there for a long time, crying. . . . Such an opportunity was almost more than I'd prayed or hoped for in many years."[11] And in 1948–1949 she hit rock bottom when agents started booking her into saloons without telling her what kind of places they were. "It hurt," she said. Some of the more respectable nightclub owners would not employ her, and these included Barney Josephson. In 1938 he opened Café Society, a New York showcase in Greenwich Village for African American talent. Billie Holiday first sang "Strange Fruit" there, and it was at this club that Josephson helped launch the careers of Lena Horne and Hazel Scott. But he had no time for Ethel, especially, it seemed, when she was at her lowest. Josephson may have broken down racial barriers and assisted the careers of dozens of African American artistes, but he was downright nasty to Ethel. In spite of her achievements and her influence on younger singers such as Billie and Lena, he refused to employ her and described her as an "Uncle Tom."[12]

It was during this period that one of her fans, Michael Alexander, saw her perform at the Club Barron in Harlem. Michael had previously been taken as a child to see Ethel in *Mamba's Daughters*:

> After a stint in the British army I returned to New York to resume my acting career. One of my colleagues in a 1948 off-Broadway production of an Agatha Christie play was Sidney Poitier, at that time a totally unknown Sidney Poitier, playing the tiny part of a Nubian steward on a Nile steamer. We were roughly the same age, and had both spent our early years in the Bahamas. Sidney was working hard to get rid of his West Indian accent, while I was struggling to hang on to my British one. We had a lot of laughs over this and we became very friendly. One of his mates was Harry Belafonte. He'd just got his first break in New York supporting Ethel Waters at the Club Barron in Harlem. He was terrified of her! Sidney and I went to their opening night to give Harry some moral support, and we were delighted when Harry made a real success with his songs in the first half. Then, after an interval, Miss Waters came on. Her appearance was a shock. In the few years since I'd last seen her she'd grown immensely stout, and her hair was completely grey, which made her look far older than her fifty-two years. Then she began to sing and I can remember exactly which number it was that first had us all cheering. It was Eubie Blake's "You're Lucky to Me," which she had introduced in Lew Leslie's *Blackbirds* in 1930. When she got to the end of that number, the audience at the Club Barron could hardly contain itself. From then on she slayed us with one old favourite after another. I met her only once. That night at the Club Barron she talked to Sidney Poitier and me for a few minutes after her performance and it was a thrill but awe-inspiring. Rather like being spoken to by a monument.[13]

Notes

1. Martin Bauml Duberman, *Paul Robeson* (London: Bodley Head, 1989), 259–60.

2. Thomas Cripps, *Slow Fade to Black: The Negro in American Film, 1900–1942* (Oxford: Oxford University Press, 1977), 384.

3. Ethel Waters with Charles Samuels, *His Eye Is on the Sparrow* (New York: Da Capo, 1992), 257–58.

4. David Shipman, *The Great Movie Stars: The Golden Years* (London: Hamlyn, 1970), 465.

5. James Baldwin, *The Devil Finds Work* (London: Joseph, 1976), 103–4.

6. Lena Horne with Richard Schickel, *Lena* (London: Deutsch, 1966), 136.

7. Eleanor Knowles, *The Films of Jeanette MacDonald and Nelson Eddy* (London: Barnes, 1975), 101.

8. Kenneth Barrow, *Flora: An Appreciation of the Life and Work of Dame Flora Robson* (London: Heinemann, 1981), 146.

9. Linda Dahl, *Morning Glory: A Biography of Mary Lou Williams* (Berkeley: University of California Press, 1999), 156–57.

10. Eartha Kitt, *I'm Still Here* (London: Sidgwick and Jackson, 1989), 44.

11. Waters, *Sparrow*, 266.

12. James Gavin, *Intimate Nights: The Golden Age of New York Cabaret* (New York: Grove Weidenfeld, 1991), 35.

13. Michael Alexander, interview with Stephen Bourne, August 2, 2004.

CHAPTER EIGHT

~

Pinky

In 1949 Ethel returned to Hollywood to make her first screen appearance since *Cabin in the Sky* in 20th Century Fox's *Pinky*. Six years had passed since *Cabin*, and in that short period the film careers of some of her contemporaries had either ended or declined. The late 1940s was not a good time for black women in Hollywood. For instance, Ethel's *Cabin* costar, Lena Horne, though under contract to MGM, made only brief guest appearances in *Till the Clouds Roll By* (1946) and *Words and Music* (1948). Singer and pianist Hazel Scott, a sophisticated and innovative cabaret star, had arrived in Hollywood around the same time as Ethel and Lena, but she soon found herself shunned by producers. Proud, defiant, and militant, Hazel insisted on a clause in her movie contracts stating that she was not to be cast as piano-playing maids, and for a time this worked. In films such as *Something to Shout About* (1943), *I Dood It* (1943), and *Broadway Rhythm* (1944), Hazel's chic and glamorous appearances in cabaret sequences helped change the stereotypical image of black women in films. However, her movie career ended abruptly after a memorable guest appearance in Warner Bros.' *Rhapsody in Blue* (1945), an all-star musical based on the life of George Gershwin. During the filming of Columbia's *The Heat's On* (1943) starring Mae West, Hazel went on strike and held up the production for three days. There were eight black girls dancing in Hazel's musical production number, and they were supposed to see eight black guys off to war while Hazel, dressed as a member of the WAC, performed at the piano. Hazel lost her temper when the makeup man was ordered to spray the girls' aprons with oil and dirt: "I blew sky-high. I honestly did. I said, 'How can you think that young women are going to see their sweethearts off to war wearing dirty aprons?' I finally got them paid as dress extras, and they wore their own clothes. It held up production for three days. . . . They told me I would never make another picture. I was under contract for one more, *Rhapsody in Blue*, and when that was finished, I never did make another picture in Hollywood."[1] It was Harry Cohn, head of Columbia, who ended Hazel's film career for holding up the production of *The Heat's On*. Hazel did not come back to Tinseltown.

In 1946 Butterfly McQueen ended her Hollywood career. The diminutive, squeaky-voiced supporting actress of films such as *Gone with the Wind* (1939), *Cabin in the Sky*, and *Duel in the Sun* (1946) became increasingly unhappy portraying what were described as "handkerchief heads." Butterfly's talent was often misused for stereotypical roles with racist undertones, and a good example of this is her unbilled appearance in *Mildred Pierce* (1945). After issuing a statement in which she declared she would no longer portray simpleminded maids, Butterfly walked away from her Hollywood career. Though cinema-goers missed her, Butterfly made the right decision. Shortly afterward, in 1947, the great jazz singer Billie Holiday had a miserable time making *New Orleans*. And it was Billie who, in her 1956 autobiography, *Lady Sings the Blues*, eloquently and movingly describes what it was like to suffer the pain and humiliation of playing a Hollywood maid:

> I thought I was going to play myself in it. I thought I was going to be Billie Holiday doing a couple of songs in a nightclub setting and that would be that. I should have known better. When I saw the script, I did. You just tell me one Negro girl who's made movies who didn't play a maid or a whore. I don't know any. I found out I was going to do a little singing, but I was still playing the part of a maid. I'd fought my whole life to keep from being somebody's damn maid. And after making more than a million bucks and establishing myself as a singer who had some taste and self respect, it was a drag to go to Hollywood and end up as a make-believe maid. Don't get me wrong. I've nothing against maids— or whores—whether they're black or white. My mother was a maid, a good one, one of the greatest. But . . . I didn't feel this damn part. How could I, after going through hell to keep from being one when I was twelve? . . . I never made another movie. And I'm in no hurry.[2]

Perhaps the greatest injustice of all was the waste of Hattie McDaniel's talent. Throughout the 1930s, playing outspoken, feisty maids, Hattie made one movie after another, stealing scene after scene from legendary Hollywood stars. Hattie's finest achievements were as Paul Robeson's quick-tempered but lovable wife Queenie in *Show Boat* (1936) and Scarlett O'Hara's faithful but outspoken mammy in *Gone with the Wind* (1939). The latter won her an Oscar for best supporting actress and a contract with Warner Bros. During the war she enjoyed movie star status while continuing to play comical maids, and in the 1942 Bette Davis melodrama *In This Our Life*, she was given a brief opportunity to try a strong dramatic role. But after the war, Hattie discovered that winning an Oscar meant little. In 1948 producer David O. Selznick, who had given her the role of Mammy in *Gone with the Wind*, seemed to have forgotten her when he cast the small but memorable role of the kindly theatre dresser Clara Morgan in *Portrait of Jennie*. The role was perfect for Hattie, but Selznick gave it to Maude Simmons. With a movie career that had started to decline around 1946, the end came in 1949, coinciding with a cycle of landmark films that attempted to take seriously America's "race" problem. But these had no place for Hattie, who in the eyes of Hollywood belonged to another era. The five films were *Home of the Brave* (May 1949), *Lost Boundaries* (June 1949), *Pinky* (September 1949), *Intruder in the Dust* (November 1949), and *No Way Out* (August 1950), in which Sidney Poitier made a memorable screen debut. Hattie McDaniel died in 1952 as Poitier's star began to rise. Before the end of the decade he had become one of the first black actors to achieve star status in Hollywood and the first to be nominated for a best actor Oscar (for *The Defiant Ones*, 1958).

In addition to the young Poitier, the "race problem" films also provided strong dramatic roles for several talented African American actors including James Edwards (*Home of the Brave*), Canada Lee (*Lost Boundaries*), and Juano Hernandez (*Intruder in the Dust*). During the war, a handful of black actors had been cast in small but heroic roles in war dramas. These included Kenneth Spencer (*Bataan*, 1943), Ben Carter (*Crash Dive*, 1943), Rex Ingram (*Sahara*, 1943), and Canada Lee (*Lifeboat*, 1944). Together with Ernest Anderson's law student in *In This Our Life* (1942), Dooley Wilson's piano-playing Sam in *Casablanca* (1942), and Canada Lee's memorable portrayal of a tragic boxing champ in *Body and Soul* (1947), these were more dignified and intelligent characterizations, a far cry from Stepin Fetchit's buffoons of the 1930s. But the only *starring* role given to a black actor in a Hollywood movie during this period was Uncle Remus in Walt Disney's *Song of the South* (1946), which many felt was a backward step in spite of James Baskette's engaging performance, which earned him an honorary Oscar. By the end of the 1940s the "race problem" cycle suggested a trend toward black realism in American cinema, but compromises were made, including the casting of the lead character in *Pinky*.

If a black actress had been cast in *Pinky* as the light-skinned, Southern-born Patricia "Pinky" Johnson, who passes for white while training as a nurse in the North, it might have atoned for Hollywood's almost nonexistent depiction of black women since the war. The same could be said for MGM's Technicolor remake of Show Boat (1951). However, this was not going to happen. Hollywood's "liberalism" would go only so far. From 1949 to 1959, Hollywood would make movies about the plight of black women, but they would not cast black actresses in the leading roles. Studios had their eye on the box office, not race relations. So, after Show Boat, cinema audiences saw a succession of white actresses playing black roles: Yvonne de Carlo (Band of Angels, 1957), Natalie Wood (Kings Go Forth, 1958), and Susan Kohner (Imitation of Life, 1959).

In spite of her fame and popularity, Lena Horne was overlooked for both Pinky and Show Boat, films that would have established her as a major movie star. Lena desperately wanted the parts, as she later explained in her award-winning one-woman Broadway stage show The Lady and Her Music (1981), but on reflection it is doubtful that Lena could have been convincing as a black woman who passed for white. This was the reason given by MGM producer Arthur Freed, who cast Ava Gardner in Show Boat: "You couldn't pass Lena off as white. The girl that played the part had to look white."[3]

As for Pinky, it is doubtful that Lena would have worked with Ethel again after the problems they encountered with each other on the set of Cabin in the Sky. A better choice might have been Hilda Simms, the Broadway star of the black-cast drama Anna Lucasta, produced by the American Negro Theatre company. In 1955, when she played Sidney Poitier's wife in a television play (Philco Playhouse: A Man Is Ten Feet Tall), the casting of Simms generated much controversy because she was so light skinned viewers thought Poitier's character had a white wife, something that was prohibited in American films and television in the 1950s. In the end the role of Pinky went to a whiter than white Fox contract player, Jeanne Crain. The only "whiter" actress under contract to Fox was Betty Grable. A more obvious choice would have been the beautiful, dark-haired and dark-complexioned Linda Darnell, also under contract to Fox. Linda would have been convincing as a woman of African descent, but Fox cast Jeanne Crain, presumably for shock value, because her screen persona was the pretty, wholesome girl next door in films such as State Fair (1945) and Margie (1946). Jeanne couldn't have been further from anyone's casting expectations. After all, this was a role that Lena Horne wanted. When director Elia Kazan took over the project, Jeanne had already been cast, and Kazan wasn't happy about it: "Jeanne Crain was a sweet girl, but she was like a Sunday school teacher. I did my best with her, but she didn't have any fire. The only good thing about her face was that it went so far in the direction of no temperament that you felt Pinky was floating through all of her experiences without reacting to them, which is what 'passing' is."[4]

In spite of Kazan's reservations, and perhaps because of his direction, Jeanne is very good as Pinky and makes a successful transition from her previous girl-next-door persona to the troubled, secretive, melancholy Pinky Johnson. However, *Pinky* did have one strong role for a black actress that could not be played by a white actress, not even Flora Robson in blackface. Mrs. Dicey Johnson is Pinky's grandmother, and this was the role that enabled Ethel to make her long-awaited film comeback.

Producer Darryl F. Zanuck, one of Hollywood's top moguls and a popular showman, had received the 1947 best film Oscar for *Gentleman's Agreement*, one of the first films to explore anti-Semitism in America. Starring Gregory Peck and directed by Elia Kazan, it was a popular success, though it hasn't stood the test of time. With an eye on the box office—and another Oscar—Zanuck decided to make another film about a "forbidden" subject, saying, "Let's do it again with a Negro." The result was *Pinky*, with a screenplay based on the novel *Quality*, a best seller from 1946, first serialized in *Ladies' Home Journal*. Its author, Cid Ricketts Sumner, was born in Brookhaven, Mississippi, and *Quality* grew out of the years she had spent in the South and—she felt—possibly out of the sense of responsibility inherited from her slave-owning grandparents. Zanuck never intended *Pinky* to be a realistic study of racism in America. In a memo to writer Dudley Nichols he says, "This is not a story about how to solve the Negro problem in the South or anywhere else. This is not a story particularly about race problems, segregation or discrimination. This is a story about one particular Negro girl who could easily pass as a white and who did pass for a while. This is the story of how and why she, as an individual, finally decided to be herself—a Negress."[5]

In Philip Dunne and Dudley Nichols's melodramatic screen adaptation, Pinky returns to her Southern home having spent years training to be a nurse "up North." Home is a shack in a black shantytown, where her granny, a matriarch known in the local community as Aunt Dicey, works as a washerwoman. For years she has undertaken backbreaking work to pay for her granddaughter's training. Dicey also takes care of a sick elderly white woman, Miss Em, who has a maternal respect for "Negroes." Dicey quickly realizes that her granddaughter has been passing for white, which she angrily claims is a "sin against God." After facing up to her grandmother's anger, Pinky confronts racism, an attempted rape by two drunken white men, and various other indignities before finding happiness within herself—as a black woman. After Miss Em passes away, Pinky discovers she has inherited the elderly white woman's grand house and land, a former plantation built by slaves. At the film's climax, Pinky rejects her white fiancé (and living a lie as his white wife) in favor of transforming Miss Em's home into a clinic for the local black community and a training school for black nurses. In the novel, and an earlier draft of the film script, the Ku Klux Klan burn down the house. But this is a Hollywood movie with a Hollywood ending. There is no mention of the Klan, the house survives, and the final shot captures Pinky's triumphant, smiling face.

Ethel later explained that she drew inspiration for the role of Dicey from her own grandmother, the proud, hardworking, fierce-tempered Sally Anderson. In her autobiography she acknowledges the presence in the supporting cast of another great Ethel of the American theatre: Ethel Barrymore (Miss Em). She also claims to "love" the director who was first assigned to *Pinky*: the legendary John "Jack" Ford, which was odd, considering his appalling treatment of her. Perhaps she forgave him? In his long and distinguished career, Ford had directed such classics as *Stagecoach* (1939), *The Grapes of Wrath* (1940), and *How Green Was My Valley* (1941), but Ethel was frightened of working for him. Ford was notorious for cursing his actors, including John Wayne, and Ethel claimed that he used the "shock treatment" while directing her, almost causing her to have a stroke. Zanuck was concerned about how Ford was portraying African Americans in a serious film. "Ford's Negroes were like Aunt Jemima. Caricatures. I thought we're going to get into trouble. . . . Some directors are great in one field and totally helpless in another field."[6] In his commentary for the 2005 DVD release of *Pinky*, film critic and biographer Kenneth Geist reveals that Philip Dunne told a Ford biographer "the stuff [footage] of Ford's I saw was Ethel Waters sort of moaning spirituals as she hung up the wash." Geist adds: "It reminded Dunne of such black travesties as the incorrigible screw up Stepin Fetchit. In fact, Ford had employed Fetchit in his 1935 Fox picture *Steamboat Round the Bend*, starring Will Rogers. Jack hated that old nigger woman, Zanuck rudely termed Ethel Waters, and she sure as hell hated him. He scared her next to death. Or, in Waters' words, Ford continually 'spooked' her, presumably by finding fault with her performance. Waters simply reacted to Ford's truculence with resentment and retreat."

Ford had to be replaced, and his replacement was Elia Kazan, who in 1947 won a best director Oscar for Zanuck's *Gentleman's Agreement* and had just triumphed on Broadway with *A Streetcar Named Desire*, starring Marlon Brando and Jessica Tandy. Taking over from the veteran Ford was a difficult challenge for Kazan, but Ethel turned out to be the least of his worries. His biographer, Richard Schickel, explains: "Kazan always identified, outsider to outsider as he saw it, with blacks, and soon she was responding to him with hugs and kisses and protestations of warm affection. He did not with her, with anyone, discuss 'motivation.' His technique, as always, was to help his actors find bits of business to focus on and let their feelings flow naturally from that activity. That was fine with Waters, and Kazan found Ethel Barrymore to be a delight."[7]

Kazan's sensitive direction helped Ethel and gave her confidence after the "shock treatment" she had received from John Ford. Ethel took the role of the kindhearted, God-fearing Dicey Johnson and transformed what could have been a one-dimensional mammy stereotype, a "handkerchief head," into a warm, dignified human being. Donald Bogle comments: "Compromises aside, where *Pinky* shone through with brilliance was Ethel Waters' moving portrayal. . . . she burns with humanity. . . . she exhibited ambiguities and contradictions that seemed to come from her own personal experience. . . . Her performance spelled the death of the one-sided mammy figure."[8]

Elia Kazan was unhappy with *Pinky* and claimed only his first film, *A Tree Grows in Brooklyn* (1945), to be the best among his early efforts. Several of his post-*Pinky* films, including *A Streetcar Named Desire* (1951) and *On the Waterfront* (1954), for which he won his second Oscar, eclipsed his earlier work. Reflecting on *Pinky* and, in particular, Darryl F. Zanuck, he is quoted by Kenneth Geist in the DVD commentary: "Zanuck would take all social issues and work them into a love story, a personal story that could carry the social story and bury the message, though both stories were predictable ones. They did not have the quality of life that I looked for in a script."

Kazan's dismissive view of *Pinky* ("it was a pastiche, taking a subject that was dynamite and castrating it") in various biographies and his own autobiography undermines the film's importance. His view is shared by others, including Kenneth Geist. *Pinky* does lack the documentary realism of Clarence Brown's superior *Intruder in the Dust*, also released in 1949, and as a Hollywood drama about racism it is not in the same class as *No Way Out*, made the following year, but neither Kazan or Geist mention *Pinky* in relation to other Hollywood films of the period that depicted black characters in the American South. These invariably featured racial stereotypes and offered cinema audiences unreal, sentimental views of the "Old South" and race relations. *Gone with the Wind*, with its devoted slaves, had been made just ten years before *Pinky*, and *Song of the South*, with Uncle Remus telling delightful stories about Brer Rabbit and singing "Zip a Dee Doo Dah," was released just three years earlier in 1946. Compared with these movies, *Pinky* is a radical departure for Hollywood, in spite of its compromises and casting of a white actress in the lead. Some white liberals and African

Americans have dismissed the film because a white actress played *Pinky*, but for those of us who are mixed race or come from biracial families, Jeanne Crain's appearance has a ring of truth because she looks white but doesn't come from an all-white family. One of the few commentators to highlight the film's strengths is Thomas Cripps:

> Despite Kazan's worst fears *Pinky* turned out as a passably good commercial expression of the conscience-liberal formula. . . . In fact, long before the NAACP's *Brown vs. Topeka Board* case called attention to the courtroom as civil rights arena, Pinky spoke for her black community by carrying its interests into the dramatic setting of a Southern courthouse. Moreover, she did so without trotting out the gothic stereotypes that passed for white Southerners in most movies. And though they did not shoot on location as Kazan, for one, wished, they neatly caught a Southern mood in everything from dress extras to local color sets. More than anything, *Pinky* offered a plot in which something *black* was at stake.[9]

As for Kazan, working with Ethel Waters was a memorable experience, and for the actress it was a rare opportunity to work with a film director who was supportive and understanding. There were very few directors in Hollywood in the 1940s who shared Kazan's respect for black actors. Vincente Minnelli was another exception. One of the worst examples is Sam Wood, who just a few years before *Pinky* was hostile toward Flora Robson, a white actress in blackface, on the set of *Saratoga Trunk* (see chapter 7). Remembering Ethel, Kazan remarks: "The most memorable thing about making that picture was the party at the end of shooting. Ethel Waters had been so sweet, kissing me all the time and telling me how much she loved me and how grateful she was to me. She and I got drunk, and I said, 'Ethel, you don't really like any white man do you?' And she said, 'I don't like any of them. I'd never trust any of 'em.' When she got drunk she told the truth, and I liked her better for it. I thought, 'I don't blame her. I can understand that.'"[10]

The five films in the "race problem" cycle were all well received by film critics, but *Pinky* was the biggest moneymaker, trailing *Jolson Sings Again* as the annual top moneymaking film of 1949. None of the other "race problem" films appeared in the top twenty. Subsequent films with "passing for white" themes also did well at the American box office, including MGM's *Show Boat*, which trailed *David and Bathsheba* as the top moneymaker of 1951, and Universal's *Imitation of Life*, which trailed *Auntie Mame*, *The Shaggy Dog*, and *Some Like It Hot* in 1959.

Pinky did not repeat the success of Zanuck and Kazan's *Gentleman's Agreement* at the Academy Awards. There was no best picture nomination. That year the Oscar went to *All the King's Men*, with nominations to *Battleground* and *The Heiress*, as well as two 20th Century Fox productions rated higher than *Pinky* by the studio: *A Letter to Three Wives* and *Twelve O'Clock High*. However, Jeanne Crain *was* nominated for best actress, a triumph for the young star who had defied her critics and transformed herself from girl next door to a capable dramatic performer. She lost out to Olivia de Havilland, whose superb portrayal of Catherine Sloper in *The Heiress* was the right choice for the award that year. The other nominees were Susan Hayward (*My Foolish Heart*), Deborah Kerr (*Edward My Son*), and Loretta Young (*Come to the Stable*). The two Ethels, Barrymore and Waters, were both nominated for best supporting actress. They both deserved to win, but the veteran actresses probably split the vote, as did fellow nominees Celeste Holm and Elsa Lanchester, who were both nominated for *Come to the Stable*. The winner was newcomer Mercedes McCambridge (*All the King's Men*), one of the rare occasions an Oscar was given to an actor for a screen debut. Ethel's nomination was the second given to a black artiste. The first had been Hattie McDaniel, who won as best supporting actress for *Gone with the Wind* in 1939. The first nominations in the leading categories were given to Dorothy Dandridge (*Carmen Jones*, 1954) and Sidney Poitier (*The Defiant Ones*, 1958), but Hattie and Ethel were the Academy's first black nominees. In 1947 James Baskette was awarded a Special Oscar for his portrayal of Uncle Remus in *Song of the South*. For the record, Ethel did not attend the 1949 Academy Award ceremony on March 23, 1950, at the RKO Pantages Theatre in Hollywood, for she had made a triumphant return to the Broadway stage in her biggest theatre success, *The Member of the Wedding*.

Notes

1. Hazel Scott, "Yoruba Is the Tribe of the Drum," in *Notes and Tones: Musician-to-Musician Interviews*, ed. Arthur Taylor (New York: Da Capo, 1993), 266.

2. Billie Holiday with William Dufty, *Lady Sings the Blues* (New York: Doubleday, 1956), 115–18.

3. Arthur Freed and John Kobal, *People Will Talk: Personal Conversations with the Legends of Hollywood* (London: Aurum Press, 1986), 389.

4. Jeff Young, *Kazan on Kazan* (London: Faber and Faber, 1999), 54.

5. Rudy Behlmer, ed., *Memo from Darryl F. Zanuck: The Golden Years at Twentieth Century-Fox* (New York: Grove Press, 1993), 162.

6. Mel Gussow, *Darryl F. Zanuck: "Don't Say Yes Until I Finish Talking"* (New York: Da Capo, 1980), 151.

7. Richard Schickel, *Elia Kazan: A Biography* (New York: HarperCollins, 2005), 204.

8. Donald Bogle, *Toms, Coons, Mulattoes, Mammies and Bucks: An Interpretive History of Blacks in American Films* (New York: Bantam, 1974), 214–18.

9. Thomas Cripps, *Making Movies Black: The Hollywood Message Movie from World War II to the Civil Rights Era* (New York: Oxford University Press, 1993), 236.

10. Young, *Kazan on Kazan*, 54–55.

~

CHAPTER NINE

A Natural Phenomenon
like Niagara Falls

In 1940, when she was only twenty-three, Carson McCullers's first novel, *The Heart Is a Lonely Hunter*, created a literary sensation. Since that time she has been celebrated as one of America's superlative writers. Before her death in 1967, Carson had written four more novels, two plays, some short stories, and a few poems. A recurring theme in all her work was also the theme of her life: loneliness, an inability to sustain deep emotional relationships, and the conflicting need for such relationships. As a writer, Carson joined an elite group from the American South, called the "Gothic School" by Tennessee Williams. The "School" also included such gifted writers as Truman Capote and William Faulkner.

Carson's 1946 novel, *The Member of the Wedding*, focused on an adolescent girl's painful transition to adulthood in America's Deep South. "Rarely has emotional turbulence been so delicately conveyed," said the *New York Times* (March 30, 1946). A few years later, when Carson adapted her novel for the stage, she described it as a play about identity and the will to belong. "It is an inward play and the conflicts are inward," she said. The play's central character is a motherless child: Frankie Adams, an awkward twelve-year-old social outcast who is unable to accept her brother's impending marriage. Her constructed "family" include two other "misfits": her soft-spoken six-year-old cousin John Henry and the African American family cook, Berenice Sadie Brown. In spite of Frankie's bullying of him, John Henry is devoted to her and unselfconsciously parades around the kitchen, where most of the action is set, wearing a woman's hat and high heels and carrying a purse. Berenice is a surrogate mother to the two children, a tower of strength who takes great care of their emotional needs.

After Carson adapted her novel for the stage, Ethel was the obvious choice for the role of Berenice, but when the actress was approached, she turned down the part. Ethel said it was a "dirty play" and that Berenice was an ugly creature who had lost her faith in God. At the time the offer was made, Ethel had hit rock bottom in her professional career (the offer for *Pinky* came afterward), and she desperately needed a job. When she read the first draft of the play, she said she was not "*that* down." Later, when Carson gave a rare television interview in a panel discussion on drama called *Lamp unto My Feet* (August 19, 1958), she said:

> Miss Waters declined the role of Berenice when she was approached for the part on the grounds that there was no mention of God in the play and that it used foul language. When it was offered her again, she reconsidered, for the producer Robert Whitehead insisted that the play did have spiritual meaning. He agreed, however, that if there were objectionable lines she could work that problem out with the director. He also assured her that the play would be a great success at the box office and that she would be making a mistake if she did not accept the role. Miss Waters was not convinced of the play's spiritual qualities until she saw the profound impact it had upon its audiences.[1]

Ethel eventually accepted the role, joining a cast that also included Julie Harris as Frankie and a scene-stealing newcomer named Brandon de Wilde as John Henry. Brandon was a seven-year-old child who had never acted before. He had been discovered at the last minute when a suitable professional child actor could not be found. He was, in fact, the son of the actor originally cast as Frankie's brother Jarvis. According to Julie Harris, "We rehearsed downtown in some dinky theatre, and there wasn't much heat. And the play, after all, took place in August, in Georgia—terribly hot. Brandon was so adorable. And Ethel, of course, was a Stage Mother, taking care of both of us. She was wonderful to work with; I adored her. The rehearsal period was a time of great joy for everybody."[2] However, difficulties with Ethel soon surfaced. In rehearsals, director Harold Clurman found her impossible. He said directing her was more like "training a bear," mainly because Ethel, in her most challenging stage role, had trouble learning her lines:

> At first, young Brandon prompted Miss Waters on her lines, and she flashed him an embarrassed smile. But the prodding soon got on her nerves, and she finally frowned fiercely at him and said, "Now, honey, I don't want you to bother me any more." The child held his tongue. . . . The night of the Philadelphia

opening [December 22, 1949], Clurman noticed that Miss Waters was more ag-
itated than usual. Everyone knew that she still did not know her lines. Aware
of her state and eager to console her, Clurman said, "You're only nervous, Ethel.
You'll be wonderful tonight—just don't worry about a thing." "You're very reas-
suring, Mr. Clurman, but I'm not reassured," she countered. She had terrible
cramps, she told him; then she went on to explain that when a black actress
faced an audience, her responsibility was greater than that of a white actress.
She had to succeed, and, indeed, she was nervous, she admitted. . . . The night
they opened in Philadelphia, Miss Waters recalled that she said her prayers as
usual and then told herself: "I'm gonna walk out there and say everything just
the way I feel it." Ethel Waters did just that, and according to the out-of-town
critics, she gave a superb performance.[3]

Celebrated dramatist Tennessee Williams was in the audience in Philadelphia. He was a Southerner who originated from Columbus, Mississippi. After the performance, he went backstage to ask Ethel for her autograph. She
told him it was she who should be requesting *his* autograph. Williams
protested, and finally Ethel took him in hand, "Honey, I'm not from the
South, but I can keep this up as long as you can!" In her autobiography, Ethel
describes *Member* as "a peculiar play, having no big climaxes or sweeping
movement. But it did capture a universal emotion in an adolescent, the feeling of being alone and wanting to belong to the world. And it was written
with tenderness and great beauty. . . . [I was] free to give my own interpretation, the character of Berenice satisfied me. She had been buffeted plenty,
but now she was not without humour, and she had retained her faith in God.
Besides this, she was moved and guided always by the memory of her one
great love for a husband who was dead."[4]

The Member of the Wedding opened at New York's Empire Theatre on January 5, 1950, and after the final curtain, an enthusiastic, cheering audience
threw their programs and hats into the air. Ethel, Julie, and Brandon were
given a standing ovation for Carson McCullers's unconventional drama, and
the next day long lines formed at the box office. Reviews were almost unan-
imously favorable. In the *New York Times* Brooks Atkinson said the play had
"incomparable insight, grace and beauty," while William Hawkins reported
in the New York *World Telegram*: "I have never heard what happened last
night at the curtain calls . . . when hundreds cried out as if with one voice
for Ethel Waters and Julie Harris."

After a long absence, Ethel had returned to Broadway in triumph. This
was her biggest critical and commercial success on the American stage.
Ethel's portrayal of Berenice placed her at the forefront of America's great
stage actresses, and she was often mentioned in the same category as Ethel

Barrymore, Katharine Cornell, Lynne Fontanne, and Helen Hayes, who were acknowledged as the "first ladies" of American theatre. For many years Ethel was the only black actress who could be found in theatre encyclopedias. However, she dismissed claims that she was "great." Untrained and without the vast experience of Barrymore, Cornell, Fontanne, and Hayes, Ethel explained that she relived from her own experiences the roles she played. In the case of the stage version of *Member*, it proved to be emotionally draining:

> You take that scene people still talk about where I sit at the table telling the children about the death of Ludie, the one man Berenice had ever loved. The one man who'd ever made her truly happy. The children keep asking Berenice questions, but her mind is way back to when Ludie died. She sits there at the kitchen table and *relives* her own agony. Ludie was dead. I was playing the woman who had loved him so dearly and who had tried to bring back his strength through her own. But to me, Ethel Waters, as I sat at that table though all those hundreds of performances on and off Broadway, it wasn't a man I grieved for. It was my own precious little grandmother, Sally Anderson, who died of cancer and I was with her. It was her death I *relived* on that stage. I remember her death as though it happened last night. . . . That's why I say when people try to tell me I'm a great actress (though I appreciate their feelings)—I say, I've just got a good memory![5]

Though Ethel remained a source of pride in the urban African American community, high ticket prices prevented many African Americans from seeing her in *Member*. Broadway was a luxury few of them could afford. However, a young student named Edward Mapp was determined to see the production. He recalls:

> *The Member of the Wedding* was a big surprise to me when it came to Broadway. I had just started as a college under-graduate student and I was going to the theatre. In those days if you didn't have money—and you were young—you would go as high up as you could go into the second balcony because you could just afford it. I remember it was only a dollar twenty and my vision was good, being young. I didn't mind going up without oxygen to the top level [laughs]. And Ethel was magnificent. The stage presence that she had. Even from the balcony you could see it. That moment when she cuddles Julie Harris and Brandon de Wilde on her lap and sings "His Eye Is on the Sparrow" was unforgettable. My respect for her increased. It is one thing to be in a film like *Cabin in the Sky* where they can film several takes until they get what they want, but it's a different matter when you're on that stage every night, in a long run, and repeating that performance over and over again. You have to have what it takes. She had a quiet presence because in that play Julie Harris's char-

acter was all over the place. She was hyper-active. In contrast, Ethel was this solid, quiet, deep, motherly figure that filled up the stage. It was a breakthrough for a black actress. She was magnificent and it was a thrill to see her photo on the cover of the theatre programme.[6]

After *Member* closed on Broadway on March 17, 1951, at the end of a run that lasted more than a year and 501 performances, the cast undertook a long, successful road tour before traveling to Hollywood to make a screen version. Independent producer Stanley Kramer had bought the screen rights, and Fred Zinnemann was scheduled to direct. He later said that was his favorite film, and this was the director who made such classics as *From Here to Eternity* (1953), *The Nun's Story* (1959), *A Man for all Seasons* (1966), and *Julia* (1977):

> Julie and Brandon were new to the screen but had very little trouble adapting to it. As for Ethel, she was so firmly wedded to her mechanics that she needed enormous persuasion to make a change. . . . Sometimes, when I insisted, she would look heavenward and say, "God is my director!" (How do you follow that one?) But she was warm, loving and generosity itself. No longer young, she would sit in her dressing room between set-ups, sometimes humming softly to herself, sometimes playing records on her portable phonograph—her own songs, mostly. . . . Ethel Waters, with her mother-earth quality and her warmth and reassurance, was a rock of Gibraltar, a haven for the tormented Frankie. The end of the second act, when the three sing "His Eye Is on the Sparrow," is one of the most moving scenes I have witnessed. (I say "witnessed" not "directed.") . . . . It has always been my favourite picture, perhaps because it is not entirely my own—or perhaps because of the quality of pure love that seems to radiate from it so strongly.[7]

For the second time in her career, Ethel transferred a memorable stage performance to the big screen, this time in an American film classic that has shamefully been overlooked in histories of cinema. Says Louis D. Giannetti in his perceptive analysis:

> *The Member of the Wedding* is one of the neglected minor masterpieces of the American cinema. A work of delicate subtlety, it was unsuccessful in its first commercial run and is seldom revived to this day, though many reviewers are charmed by the work on those rare occasions when it is revived. Furthermore, with the exception of Pauline Kael, who has praised the movie enthusiastically, most critics have ignored it, or have dismissed it as mere canned theatre, since the script is virtually a transcription of the stage play. . . . One of the most moving scenes in the film is that in which she [Berenice] ritualistically re-

counts the details of Ludie's death to the two awed youngsters. The scene is powerfully conveyed. Temporarily abandoning his documentary visual style, Zinnemann shoots the scene from a low angle, gradually moving into a tight close-up of Berenice's tear-streaked face. She is totally oblivious of her surroundings, conscious only of the anguish and solitude of her life since Ludie's death. The lights are stylized expressionistically, plunging the three vulnerable creatures into an ethereal twilight.[8]

In Britain, film critic Dilys Powell saluted Julie Harris's "superb performance" [in the *Sunday Times*], adding that her "extraordinary understanding of the restlessness, the uncertainty and the violence of closing childhood" made her forget that she was too old for the part.[9] And though *The Member of the Wedding* had universal appeal, it influenced a whole generation of lesbians who, says Joan Nestle, cofounder of New York's Lesbian Herstory Archives, "identified with the forlorn little tomboy played so well by Julie Harris. A postcard of Julie resting on Ethel's ample bosom was very popular and still is in lesbian homes. The whole world surrounding Carson McCullers, her home in Brooklyn with Truman Capote and Gypsy Rose Lee and Tennessee Williams from time to time, I think, was homoerotic."[10]

Julie Harris's portrayal of Frankie earned her a best actress Oscar nomination, but she lost out to another celebrated performance that transferred from Broadway to Hollywood that year: Shirley Booth in *Come Back, Little Sheba*. Ethel should have been nominated, and many books claim that she received her second Academy Award nomination for *Member*. However, she is not in the lineup. In addition to Booth and Harris, the 1952 nominees were Bette Davis, Joan Crawford, and Susan Hayward. In 2001, Harris warmly reflected on Ethel and their association:

When I saw her in *Mamba's Daughters* and *Cabin in the Sky*, I thought "That's what I want to be. That's the greatest actress I've ever seen." It would remain so, except for Laurette Taylor [in *The Glass Menagerie*]. Ethel Waters was one of the greatest actors I ever saw in my life. I said, "That's what it's all about." I've seen a lot of great actresses onstage—Laurette Taylor, Irene Worth, Ruth Gordon, Wendy Hiller, and now Janet McTeer. Ethel was a supreme actress because she had such power. I used to think she was a natural phenomenon like Niagara Falls. She was glorious and she was true and she was funny. When I heard her sing certain songs, I'd say, "Now I know what the meaning of cute is. Sometimes, Ethel, you are just so cute." It was her humor. It was her smile. It was the way she wrapped her humor around things. She was adorable. She was also shockingly tragic, like the face of Michelangelo. She was really much larger than life and just glorious—and always so true.[11]

Notes

1. Virginia Spencer Carr, *The Lonely Hunter: A Biography of Carson McCullers* (New York: Doubleday, 1975), 471–72.

2. William and Jane Stott, *On Broadway* (London: Thames and Hudson, 1979), 155.

3. Spencer Carr, *Lonely Hunter*, 334–35.

4. Ethel Waters with Charles Samuels, *His Eye Is on the Sparrow* (New York: Da Capo, 1992), 274.

5. Ethel Waters, *To Me It's Wonderful* (New York: Harper and Row, 1972), 134.

6. Edward Mapp, interview with Stephen Bourne, London, August 15, 2005.

7. Fred Zinnemann, *Fred Zinnemann: An Autobiography* (London: Bloomsbury, 1992), 114–15.

8. Louis D. Giannetti, *Literature/Film Quarterly* 4, no. 1 (Winter 1976), 28–38.

9. Quoted in David Shipman, *The Great Movie Stars: The International Years* (London: Angus and Robertson, 1972), 227.

10. Joan Nestle, letter to Stephen Bourne, February 10, 1994. Reproduced with permission.

11. Jackson R. Bryer and Richard A. Davison, eds., *The Actor's Art: Conversations with Contemporary American Stage Performers* (New Brunswick: Rutgers University Press, 2001), 93.

Author's note: Ethel made further appearances in The Member of the Wedding, *notably at the Congress Hall, Berlin (September 1957), under the auspices of the United States State Department, and at the Pasadena Playhouse, California (February 1964). There have been several American television adaptations of* The Member of the Wedding, *including 1958 (CBS), with Claudia McNeil as Berenice, directed by Robert Mulligan (who later directed the 1962 screen version of Harper Lee's* To Kill a Mockingbird*); 1982 (NBC), with Pearl Bailey; and 1997 (USA Network), with Alfre Woodard. In Britain in 1957, Bertice Reading recreated her Royal Court stage performance as Berenice for BBC television. In 1960 Vinnette Carroll starred in a second British television adaptation (for ITV). In 1973 jazz singer Cleo Laine made a rare excursion into drama when she played Berenice in a BBC radio version.*

CHAPTER TEN

~

Ethel on the Etherwaves

The title for this chapter has been borrowed from Henry T. Sampson's *Swingin' on the Etherwaves* (see bibliography), an exhaustive and invaluable two-volume survey of African Americans in radio and television covering the period 1925 to 1955.[1] I am adapting Sampson's title for this chapter because his research confirms that Ethel was one of the pioneers of both mediums in America.

The earliest entry for Ethel in Sampson's chronology is a report from *Negro World* dated August 30, 1930: "Colored radio stars give novel cabaret party." A month earlier, on July 29 in Chicago, Ethel had participated in an "All Negro Hour Club" broadcast from the radio station WSBC. In May, 1933, she made a guest appearance on the *Rudy Vallee Show*, and *Variety* (May 27, 1933) noted: "Miss Waters limited her offering to 'Stormy Weather.' If there was such a thing as a record of response for encores, Miss Waters would have encored all night. No colored woman has yet reached prominence on the radio, commercially or otherwise. If that's ever done, Miss Waters will probably be the first to do it." A second entry for that year acknowledges another landmark in her career. On July 1, 1933, Ethel, then starring at the Cotton Club, signed a contract to broadcast twice weekly over the NBC network, becoming the first black woman artist to have a regular radio show over a major network. Her theme song on the air was "Stormy Weather." She was heard every Monday and Wednesday evening at 11:00. Another program featuring Ethel was enthusiastically reviewed by Vere E. Johns in the *New York Age* (November 14, 1933): "We love to remember the great departed Florence Mills, but we need not worry so much now, for a right worthy successor to La Mills is here—Ethel Waters." In 1934 Ethel began negotiations to sign a contract with the American Oil Company to broadcast over the CBS network, but radio stations in Georgia and Florida objected on the grounds that a white orchestra should not play for a black singer, not even over the radio, and negotiations ended.

In spite of occasional encounters with racism in the radio industry, Ethel did make many radio appearances throughout the 1930s and 1940s as a singer, and some of the highlights recorded by Sampson include *A Song of Thanksgiving* (November 27, 1935), with the Hall Johnson and Eva Jessye choirs; *Bing Crosby Show* (June 19, 1940), for which she was praised by Ben Gross, radio editor of the *Daily News*: "Whether singing the latest hot numbers or a tender spiritual, she conveys to the listener the very soul of the song. Her combination of delicacy, humor, and dramatic power are breathtaking"; *Jubilee* (September 1, 1941), with Duke Ellington and the Hall Johnson Choir; *Command Performance* (December 24, 1942), with Bob Hope, Bing Crosby, Dorothy Lamour, Cary Grant, Dinah Shore, and Red Skelton (this program was reported to be the most expensive radio production ever made, and its purpose was to forge for that evening a link between the servicemen abroad and Americans at home); and *Harlem Amateur Hour* (November 18, 1952), with Lucky Millender and Dizzy Gillespie, broadcast from the Apollo Theatre in New York, on which Ethel sang "St. Louis Blues."

Ethel was also a television pioneer, though she was not the first to appear in the medium. The first black person to appear before a television camera was African American cabaret entertainer Nina Mae McKinney, but this historic event did not happen in America. On February 17, 1933, Nina visited John Logie Baird's experimental television studio in central London to take part in an early transmission. The legendary Josephine Baker, on a rare visit to London, made a similar appearance on October 4, 1933. A photograph of Josephine at the studio, wearing a striped blazer and black skirt, has survived. By the time Ethel made a historic appearance in an experimental television program in New York in 1939, African Americans had already been taking part in the medium—in Britain.[2]

The British Broadcasting Corporation (BBC) officially opened its regular, high-definition television service at Alexandra Palace in north London on November 2, 1936, and some of its prewar music and variety shows featured a number of black entertainers who were then starring on the London stage, mostly in musicals, revues, and nightclubs. These included Buck and Bubbles (in a variety show on the opening day), Eunice Wilson, Alberta Hunter, Valaida Snow, the Mills Brothers, Fats Waller, Paul Robeson, Elisabeth Welch, and Adelaide Hall.

In an attempt to learn how to use the new television medium, NBC turned to radio for its format and chose to adapt a commercial variety program. The result, transmitted from the NBC studios in New York, on the evening of June 14, 1939, was *The Ethel Waters Show*. The bill included several variety acts as well as Ethel, who along with African American actresses Fredi Washington and Georgette Harvey performed a dramatic sequence from her hit play *Mamba's Daughters*. Said *Variety* (June 28, 1939), referring to the medium as "visio": "Standout on the bill was an extract from the recent Broadway play *Mamba's Daughters* with Ethel Waters playing the part that won her such praise from critics and audiences last winter. Although the isolated first scene of the third act necessarily lacked clarity and cohesion without proper buildup and explanation, Miss Waters' performance was glowingly simple and sincere and raised the sketch to an affecting emotional pitch. To put over that kind of inner-felt underplaying was a demonstration of visio's possibilities as well as thrilling performance." A photograph of Ethel and fellow cast members on the studio floor, performing in the telecast in front of cameras, can be seen in volume 1 of Henry T. Sampson's *Swingin' on the Etherwaves*. For the record, in Britain, the first black actresses to appear on television were Pauline Henriques and Connie Smith in Eugene O'Neill's *All God's Chullun' Got Wings*. This was transmitted live from the BBC's Alexandra Palace studios on September 16, 1946.

During the war, in 1944, Ethel participated in another historic production, this time for BBC radio. It was a rare opportunity for Ethel to play a dramatic role, and it proved to be one of her most rewarding assignments. Paul Robeson had based himself in Britain from 1928 (when he appeared in the London stage version of *Show Boat*) until the outbreak of the Second World War in 1939, when he returned to America with his family. Throughout his career, Robeson frequently appeared on radio programs broadcast by the BBC, and at the height of his popularity in 1937, he was voted Britain's most popular radio singer. In 1944 Robeson took part as the speaker of the prologue in a now-forgotten—and lost—BBC radio broadcast, a "ballad-opera" by Langston Hughes called *The Man Who Went to War*. It was first broadcast in America on February 20, and then in Britain on March 6 (from records made from the American broadcast). Robeson turned down the lead, Johnny Lee, because he was then appearing on Broadway in *Othello*, and he was concerned about straining his voice. This part was taken by Canada Lee. Ethel was cast as his wife, Sally. Inexplicably, this landmark production is not mentioned in any of the numerous books about Robeson. Though a photograph of him with cast members Ethel, Canada Lee, Hall Johnson, and folk singer Josh White (who sang the narration) is featured in Susan Robeson's pictorial biography of her grandfather, *The Whole World in His Hands* (1981), the author does not mention the production in the caption or text. The cast were brought together in New York by one of the BBC's top radio producers, D. G. Bridson, and he invited Langston Hughes to write the script. The following extract, taken from Bridson's autobiography, gives us some insight into the significance of this forgotten production, which brought together some of the most important African Americans of wartime America:

> My plan was to write a simple sort of folk-tale round the lives of a man and his wife in a town like London during the war. But though their story would be London's own, the town itself—like the man and his wife—would not be English, but Negro. The man joins up and goes to fight the war with his friends; his wife goes to work in a war factory and suffers all the terrors of the Blitz. . . . The impact of the work in performance was incredibly moving. Ethel Waters' parting from her husband and her singing of *Sometimes I feel like a motherless child* almost stopped the show in the studio. The performances of Canada Lee and Paul Robeson, the rousing songs in the troop-train. . . . As a gesture of friendship from one people to another, *The Man Who Went to War* was probably unique. As a prophetic echo of the Negro's post-war struggle for Civil Rights, it might have been a timely warning. Either way, it was quite one of the most popular broadcasts I ever had on the air, being heard in Britain by nearly ten million listeners on its first transmission alone.[3]

Bridson explains in his autobiography that the recording made by the BBC was promptly destroyed after its second broadcast in Britain "by some fool of a BBC administrator." It was many years later that the only surviving discs were discovered in America. They were taken into the BBC's New York office for copying onto a tape that could be sent to Bridson in London. Instead of being copied, the actual discs were shipped to Bridson, and—as the program had been recorded on fragile wartime stock (cut on a glass base)—they reached him "in a thousand fragments. And that was the end of *The Man Who Went to War*." But not quite.

The Langston Hughes Estate have given permission for a short extract to be included in this book. I have chosen the air raid scene, in which Langston Hughes effectively captured the tension and terror experienced by those under fire on the home front in Britain. It is an extraordinary sequence because Hughes and the American home front did not have direct experience of air raids. The cast included Ethel as Sally, Osceola Archer as Mrs. Johnson, Cherokee Thornton as Grandpa, Theodora Smith as Lottie, William Johnson as Jerry, and Melvin Green as the warden:

MRS. JOHNSON: Sounds like a heavy raid doesn't it? I thought they'd be over again tonight.

SALLY: They always come when it's a full moon.

GRANDPA: Danged old planes—and me down here in the shelter helpless as a cooter. I'd like to fill them full of buckshot.

SALLY: All right Grandpa. You save your breath.

WHISTLE OF BOMB FALLING: EXPLOSION

LOTTIE: (SOBS) Oh, why don't they go away? Night after night they come back.

SALLY: There, there, honey. Don't you cry, now. Crying won't keep them away. Try and go to sleep, then you won't hear them.

LOTTIE: (STILL SOBBING) I can't go to sleep. I've not slept since we were bombed out. I'm scared.

SALLY: Shhh! Don't take on so, honey! You'll make yourself sick.

LOTTIE: (SOBS) If it'd been your house they'd hit. I was trying to go to sleep when the bomb came. . . . I didn't know. (BREAKS DOWN)

MRS. JOHNSON: We know, honey—but you're here now, ain't you? Safe and sound?

LOTTIE: (SOBS) I want my Joe.

SALLY: You mustn't talk about it now! Not now! You'll frighten the children, darlin'.

LOTTIE: (SOBS) I'm sorry, Sally. I'll try not to.

WHISTLE OF ANOTHER BOMB

JERRY: Mama! Mama! Maybe that hit *our* house.

SALLY: We don't know what it hit, son.

GRANDPA: Now, Jerry. You keep quiet, like a man. Baby isn't crying.

JERRY: Baby don't know what it's all about. I do. I wish I had a gun, too.

GRANDPA: Now if *I'd* got a gun—would I be down here in the shelter?

BEHIND SPEECH THE HALL JOHNSON CHOIR VERY QUIETLY HAS BEGUN TO SING "CITY CALLED HEAVEN."

SALLY: Grandpa, will you stop talking about guns. There's enough noise already.

LOTTIE: (NOT CRYING ANYMORE) It makes you feel so helpless. Just sitting here, waiting and listening. That's the way it was that night.

SALLY: Sh, Lottie. Don't listen to the planes, honey. Everything'll be alright.

THE CHOIR NOW DROWNS THE QUIET CHATTER OF THE CROWD.

ABOVE THE SONG THE ALL CLEAR SOUNDS. DURING THE LAST
LINE THEY

BREAK IT UP TO SHOUT.

VOICES: There's the warden. Let the warden through. There's the all clear.

WARDEN: That's the all-clear going now. Grandpa! Sally! I've got bad news
for you.

SALLY: For us?

WARDEN: Yes, I'm sorry for you. Your house has been hit.

SALLY: Our house has been hit. What happened?

WARDEN: It just isn't there anymore.

JERRY: Mama, our house isn't there anymore?

WARDEN: No, sonny, it isn't there anymore.

GRANDPA: You mean—we've not got a home, now?

SALLY: (BEGINS TO CRY) Where shall we go? What shall we do?

MRS. JOHNSON: Now honey, you ain't alone! I ain't been your neighbour
all these years for nothing, living just down the street from you. Bring your
children and Grandpa, and you come to live with us until you get straight.
That is, if I still got a house. Warden, have I still got a house?

WARDEN: Yes, Mrs. Johnson, your home is o.k.

MRS. JOHNSON: Then come along home with me, honey, come on.

The release of *Pinky* led to a guest appearance on Ed Sullivan's popular television variety show *Toast of the Town* in 1949, and while still performing in *The Member of the Wedding* on Broadway, Ethel accepted the lead in a television comedy series, *Beulah*. This was filmed in the Bronx section of New York, and in an interview in the *Los Angeles Sentinel* (October 19, 1950), Ethel comments: "Playing both a TV and a Broadway part at the same time is tough. All day long I'm Beulah—a happy-go-lucky domestic with a talent for saying clever things. Then two hours after I finish being a kitchen queen, I take on a serious dramatic role in the theatre. I like working hard. An actress is never too old to learn. And TV—because it's so much closer and smaller than film work—is sure teaching me things."

From October 3, 1950, to September 22, 1953, ABC's *Beulah* was the first nationally broadcast weekly television series starring an African American. This half-hour situation comedy focused on a conscientious, lovable middle-aged black domestic named Beulah and the white Henderson family who employed her. According to J. Fred MacDonald, "The problems around which each episode Beulah revolved were common to the genre—invariably an honest misunderstanding which caused the protagonist to do one thing when quite another was called for. But Beulah suffered and endured. And she usually did so without complaint."[4] Ethel played Beulah until 1952. In April that year, there was a major cast change when Hollywood veteran Hattie McDaniel was scheduled to replace Ethel. Ill health prevented Hattie from appearing as Beulah, and the part went to Louise Beavers until she decided to leave the role in September 1953.

Though popular with viewers, *Beulah* came under fire from critics for perpetuating racial stereotypes. Ethel was singled out for betraying her other outstanding accomplishments on stage and in films. At its annual convention in June 1951, the National Association for the Advancement of Colored People (NAACP) condemned *Beulah* and another popular sitcom, *Amos 'n' Andy*. However, writer Hal Kanter later explains in Marlon Riggs's television documentary *Color Adjustment* (1989): "I don't think that the sponsors, or the network, and certainly not the writers ever considered the questions of race relations or stereotyping. That was the furthest from our minds. What we were trying to do was to present an amusing set of characters. Beulah was popular because she was idealized, what every person would love to have in a housekeeper."[5]

In *Color Adjustment*, cultural critic Patricia A. Turner comments: "A show like *Beulah* reinforced the notion of an African American woman comfortable working in a domestic environment, comfortable working in a white family's home with no family, no network of her own and indifferent to the needs of that," while actress Esther Rolle adds that "You made her so happy and you made her so unaware of her own children, and so aware of somebody else's children, that was the Hollywood maid. I knew a lot of people who worked as domestics, and people who had to educate their children from their earnings as domestics. And they did it because they didn't want *their* children to go through what they were going through. That's nobility." In 2001 Donald Bogle offered the following summary:

> ABC's decision to cast Ethel Waters proved a wise one. Improbable as it may seem, she truly lent the series some distinction and a lopsided credibility. Her presence also indicated—early on—that viewers might overlook weak story lines or poorly developed characters if they liked the people on-screen. Waters endowed the show with a subtext that made *Beulah* far more than it appeared on the surface. . . . Occupying a unique place in the national consciousness, Ethel Waters was perceived as a woman of emotional depth and resilience; a

woman whose spirit and drive had enabled her to endure in a sometimes tough and cruel world. . . . As played by Waters, Beulah is hard not to like. Gracing this nothing character with her own profound warmth and tenderness as well as a modicum of conviction, Waters transformed Beulah into a knowing earth mother, able to unravel life's tangled (albeit trivial) difficulties and to make everything right.[6]

Butterfly McQueen played Beulah's best friend, Oriole, who worked as a domestic for another family in the neighborhood and spent time with Beulah in the Henderson's kitchen. Butterfly did not have happy memories of working with Ethel and, in later interviews, expresses the difficulties she faced with the star: "She wasn't pleasant. I went on and sure enough, she would call me 'manure.' She'd been to the University of Hard Knocks, and so she used four-letter words. And she used another four-letter word. A bedroom word. And I was so embarrassed because there was a little girl there. And do you know who that little girl was? Leslie Uggams."[7] Butterfly claims that Ethel became jealous because she was getting all the laughs: "She was the star, and as such she used her power. The backstage atmosphere became very tense. I decided to give up the part."[8] After Butterfly left the cast, Ruby Dandridge, mother of Dorothy, took over the role of Oriole. Coincidentally, Butterfly and Ruby had appeared with Ethel in MGM's screen version of Cabin in the Sky. After Beulah ended in September 1953, there would be no regular series starring a black actress again for fifteen years (Diahann Carroll in the popular comedy series Julia).

On January 5, 1952, Ethel appeared in another radio drama, Sixteen Sticks in a Bundle, in NBC's anthology series Cavalcade of America. In this true story adapted from Farm Journal, she played Leah Young, a courageous Georgia mother who overcame all obstacles to provide her fourteen children with an education. On television she made occasional guest appearances in variety shows, but in 1954, an appearance on Edward R. Murrow's famous talk show Person to Person broke new ground. In the popular series, which was launched in 1953 and ran throughout the rest of the 1950s, journalist Murrow interviewed his celebrity guests live: Murrow in the studio with a cigarette in his hand, his guests in their homes. The list of guests is awesome: John F. Kennedy, Eleanor Roosevelt, Groucho Marx, Marilyn Monroe, Marlon Brando, Humphrey Bogart and Lauren Bacall, Noel Coward, Elizabeth Taylor and her then husband Mike Todd. To his credit, Murrow also included such African American celebrities as Duke Ellington, Cab Calloway, and Sammy Davis Jr. At the time of her interview, Ethel's career was in decline (see chapter 11), and she was living on the second floor of a redbrick house in Brooklyn's Crown Heights, hardly the expected residence of a legend. During the interview, Ethel admits she is unemployed: "There's a compulsory relaxation and then there's a voluntary relaxation. Right now I'm on the compulsory one. So while I'm waiting for the phone to ring for me to get some employment while I'm in between dates—that's the celebrity way of expressing it—I just waste away my time reminiscing." Though Murrow talks to Ethel for only fifteen minutes, he covers a lot of ground, and Ethel exposes a lot of her trouble and pain. It is heartbreaking to watch this giant looking so demoralized and uncertain about her future: "I constantly can't live in my tragic past. And it has been tragic. I have to get away from it at times because it undermines me." Donald Bogle comments:

> This was the stuff of real drama, worlds removed from everyday 1950s bland television fare. Here was a woman down on her luck, openly revealing her fears and her great vulnerabilities. Few primetime programs could ever hope to emotionally match this one, which might have been the first of television's confessional interviews; long before interviewers like Barbara Walters or Oprah Winfrey mastered the art of drawing personal stories out of their subjects. . . . Waters used the medium to speak directly and seriously to viewers. TV had known fake intimacy. But here was the real thing, unadulterated, and worlds removed from the standard *Person to Person* fare. Most such Murrow interviews were light-hearted celebrity chatter. The only other interview to touch the viewer as Waters did was Murrow's conversation with a haunting, melancholic Marilyn Monroe.[9]

Ethel landed occasional dramatic roles on television throughout the 1950s. In 1955 she played Harry Belafonte's mother in *Winner by Decision*, shown in the anthology series *General Electric Theater*, and later that year she played Dilsey in a *Playwrights '56* presentation of William Faulkner's *The Sound and the Fury*. Lillian Gish was also in the cast. However, in most of her dramatic programs, Ethel was typecast as a faithful mammy or suffering mother. Still, Donald Bogle acknowledges that Ethel occupied a unique position in American television at this time:

> She emerged as perhaps television's most distinctive and important African American star of the Eisenhower decade; not only the one African American actress immediately known by face and name to the ever-growing television audience but also the one Black actress who played a series of dramatic roles. Most significantly, Ethel Waters helped bridge the prewar and postwar eras, leading to more modern depictions of African American women. Almost always she represented, as an actress and as a personality, the strong, long-suffering Black

woman, whose purpose fundamentally was to serve, nurture, and ultimately impart wisdom. What lifted her out of the old-style mammy category was that her dramatic matriarchs could be troubled, restless, searching, clearly aware of moral choices to be made. Her important appearances—even in a half-baked production like *The Sound and the Fury* or a routine melodrama like *Winner By Decision*—altered the idea of the African American woman as a simple soul without any real reasons to sing the blues.[10]

In 1957 Ethel made a memorable guest appearance on *The Ford Show Starring Tennessee Ernie Ford*, singing "Cabin in the Sky" and joining Ford for a medley that included a lively version of "St. Louis Blues." At the end of the show Ethel joined Ford and chorus for a moving rendition of the hymn "Stand By Me." In 1958 she appeared in *The Mike Wallace Interview*. "You want to talk about money?" he asked. "Yeah. I ain't got none," Ethel replied. Three years later came an important dramatic role in *Route 66*, a popular adventure series charting the exploits of two youthful wanderers, Tod (Martin Milner) and Buz (George Maharis), traveling across country. The series ran from 1960 to 1964. The episode "Good Night, Sweet Blues" was filmed in Pittsburgh, Pennsylvania, and originally broadcast on October 6, 1961. In the story, Tod and Buz are nearly involved in a head-on highway accident with a veteran blues singer, Jennifer Henderson, or "Miss Jenny," played by Ethel, who has had a stroke in her car. Miss Jenny doesn't believe it when she is told by a doctor she is *not* dying and asks Tod and Buz to round up her old band members for a final get-together. Tod and Buz locate the elderly men just in time for her final performance, on her deathbed. Several famous jazz musicians were cast as Miss Jenny's band members, including Coleman Hawkins, Jo Jones, and Roy Eldridge. For infusing her otherwise one-dimensional character with a sense of urgency and vitality, Ethel became the first black actress to be nominated for an Emmy award. These had been presented by the Academy of Television Arts and Sciences since 1948 and were popularly known as American television's equivalent of the Oscar. In 1961–1962, Ethel was nominated in the category of outstanding single performance by a lead actress. The other nominees included Geraldine Brooks (*Bus Stop*), Suzanne Pleshette (*Dr. Kildare*), and Inger Stevens (*Dick Powell Theatre*), but the winner was Ethel's costar from *The Member of the Wedding*: Julie Harris (for *Hallmark Hall of Fame: Victoria Regina*). Before Ethel was nominated, the only black stars recognized by the Emmys had been Harry Belafonte and Sammy Davis Jr. for music and variety shows. Ethel was the first to be recognized for a dramatic role. It was in 1973–1974 that an African American actress finally won an Emmy for a leading dramatic role: Cicely Tyson for the acclaimed made-for-television movie *The Autobiography of Miss Jane Pittman*.

One final comment on Ethel and *Route 66*. In 1996 soprano Marni Nixon recalled in an interview for the BBC radio tribute *Something Wonderful* some of her famous "ghosting" jobs in classic Hollywood movie musicals. These had included Deborah Kerr in *The King and I* (1956), Natalie Wood in *West Side Story* (1961), and Audrey Hepburn in *My Fair Lady* (1964). She also described some of her other, lesser known ghosting jobs, the most surprising of which was her revelation that she had ghosted Ethel:

> They weren't always big major musicals, they were the angels in Ingrid Bergman's *Joan of Arc*, humming stanzas, a high note for Marilyn Monroe [in "Diamonds Are a Girl's Best Friend"] in *Gentlemen Prefer Blondes*, Janet Leigh singing in the bathtub, the three singing geese in the "Jolly Holiday" number in *Mary Poppins*. I even did Ethel Waters in a television show called *Route 66*. I had to imitate an early recording that she did called "I'm Coming Virginia," a very famous Ethel Waters song from the 1920s. And Ethel Waters was in the show herself, she was still alive, playing the part of a dying blues singer who listens to the early recording of "I'm Coming Virginia" on her deathbed. She couldn't sing the song as a young woman anymore, nor could they use the original recording for some technical reason. And they wanted me to record the song, with her standing behind me, coaching me, to sound just like her! That was scary. I sometimes say that Audrey Hepburn's was the hardest voice to do [in *My Fair Lady*] but of all the voices I did, Ethel Waters's was the hardest because I don't have a black sound. I don't have that bluesy feeling. It was the most difficult thing, but I could imitate from the original recording and somehow they kept it in.[11]

In the late 1960s and early 1970s, Ethel made occasional guest appearances in television variety and talk shows including *The Hollywood Palace* (1969) with a young Diana Ross, with whom she duetted on "Bread and Gravy," an old favorite of Ethel's. In 1971 Ethel, looking slimmer than she had in previous television appearances, made a lovely guest appearance on *The Pearl Bailey Show*. Pearl had admired Ethel for years, and the duo are warm and affectionate toward each other. For her solo, Ethel gave an emotional rendition of "His Eye Is on the Sparrow." Then Pearl joined her for a rousing version of "When the Trumpet Sounds," which threatened to turn the show into a revival meeting. On Johnny Carson's *Sun City Scandals '72* (1972) Ethel joined other show business veterans, such as Bette Davis, Eddie Foy Jr., and Jerry Colonna, for a variety show that consisted of musical performances and comedy sketches. To promote the publication of her second autobiography, *To Me It's Wonderful*, Ethel made an appearance on *The David Frost Show* on May 10, 1972. Ethel's sense of humor and infectious laugh shone through on the Frost show. "I've watched you a long, long time, child," she told Frost, "and you're a brilliant boy." Ethel shared with the British Frost her "cherished memories" of her visit to London in 1929 for appearances at the Palladium, Holborn Empire, and Café de Paris. She also recalled her encounter with the Prince of Wales at the Café de Paris and her friendship with one of the Café's "hostesses," Merle Oberon, just before she became a movie star. Ethel then sang "Partners with God," for which she had written the lyrics, and she was accompanied by her trusted pianist Reginald Beane. Fellow guests on *The Tonight Show Starring Johnny Carson*, which aired on October 27, 1972, included movie legend Mickey Rooney and jazz legend Artie Shaw, and it proved to be a lively event. Carson talked to Ethel about the recent (October 6) testimonial dinner in Ethel's honor, hosted by Billy Graham. The audience roared with laughter when Ethel told Carson that Graham had "picked up the tab." Rooney referred to Ethel as "Miss Waters," and Shaw told her: "Many, many years ago, when I was a young kid, and I was beginning to learn a little about music, a record of yours came out called 'Am I Blue?' and that thing just turned me on like a Christmas tree. I just lit up all over the place. I must have worn out ten of those records and this is the first time I've ever had a chance to tell you." Ethel responded by informing Carson and the audience that Shaw used to be a sex symbol, and this was greeted with loud laughter and applause. Rooney quipped, "What am I? A lampshade?" Ethel closed the show with "Cabin in the Sky."

In a special edition of *The Mike Douglas Show* (also known as *Mike in Hollywood*), which aired on February 16, 1976, Douglas promoted the release of MGM's compilation film *That's Entertainment! Part 2*. This film was the first on-screen reunion for Fred Astaire and Gene Kelly since their guest appearance in the musical extravaganza *Ziegfeld Follies* (1945). For *TE2* they copresented a series of magical sequences from some of MGM's best musicals. Ethel singing "Taking a Chance on Love" from *Cabin in the Sky* proved to be one of the most memorable. By 1976, Ethel had restricted her public appearances to Billy Graham's Crusades. Her health was deteriorating, but she readily agreed to join Mike Douglas, Fred, and Gene in the program. This was her final television appearance, recorded just eight months before her eightieth birthday. Physically frail and partially blind, Ethel nonetheless won over her host, her fellow guests, and the viewers. She began by heaping praise on Fred: "He's just grace personified. So is my boy Gene. One can appreciate the personalities of these two gentlemen if you appreciate honesty, artistry and a certain amount of humility in their dancing. They love what they do and they do it with their heart and soul. I love to see that because we don't see it anymore. We see a certain amount of flash but we don't see depth." Gene responded, "You're very kind," but Ethel explained, "No, I'm honest." Said

Mike: "It's interesting to hear this lady turn to you and say how much you convey on that screen, have you ever seen anyone with more soul and more feeling than this lady when she performs?" Fred and Gene replied no—and they had both worked with Judy Garland! Gene added: "I used to sneak in and watch her rehearse *Cabin in the Sky* and it was really inspiring." When Mike Douglas asked Ethel, "So many people come up to you and say they love you. How does that make you feel?" she replied, "Humble and grateful. I can't repeat that too often. That's something you can't buy and it's something they don't have to give you and when they do it, I'm grateful. I don't accept it as a matter of fact." There wasn't a dry eye on the set when Ethel closed the interview by singing, beautifully, with a simple piano accompaniment, "Cabin in the Sky." It was a fitting, emotional finale to Ethel's extraordinary career.

Notes

1. Henry T. Sampson, *Swingin' on the Etherwaves: A Chronological History of African Americans in Radio and Television Broadcasting, 1925–1955* (Lanham, Md.: Scarecrow Press, 2005).

2. Stephen Bourne, "A Sort of Magic: Television The First Thirty Years 1932–61," in *Black in the British Frame: The Black Experience in British Film and Television* (London: Continuum, 2001), 59–60.

3. D. G. Bridson, *Prospero and Ariel: The Rise and Fall of Radio—A Personal Recollection* (London: Gollancz, 1971), 109–11.

4. J. Fred MacDonald, *Blacks and White TV: Afro-Americans in Television since 1948* (Chicago: Nelson-Hall, 1983), 22–23.

5. *Color Adjustment* (1989), directed by Marlon Riggs and narrated by Ruby Dee, aired on public television in the early 1990s. It took an interpretive look at images of African Americans in fifty years of American television history, using footage from popular shows such as *Amos 'n' Andy*, *Julia*, and *Good Times* to compare the stereotypes in early programs with those of recent, presumably more enlightened, decades.

6. Donald Bogle, *Prime Time Blues: African Americans on Network Television* (New York: Farrar, Straus and Giroux, 2001), 23–25.

7. Tinkerbelle, "McQueen for a Day," *Andy Warhol's Interview* IV, no 11 (November 1974), 19. Singer Leslie Uggams went on to become a television star in adulthood and is best known for her role as the slave Kizzy in the epic drama *Roots* (1977).

8. Charles Stumpf, "Remembering Butterfly McQueen," *Films of the Golden Age* (Spring 1996), 53.

9. Bogle, *Prime Time Blues*, 71–73.

10. Bogle, *Prime Time Blues*, 70–71.

11. Marni Nixon, interviewed by Stephen Bourne for BBC Radio 2's *Something Wonderful* (September 22, 1996).

CHAPTER ELEVEN

~

Homeward Bound

In 1950 Ethel was honored with a dinner at New York's Park-Sheraton Hotel, given by the Harlem Business Women. Carl Van Vechten, her friend since the 1920s (see chapter 3), delivered a speech and later described the event as "the best public dinner I ever attended, really wonderful, and Ethel was marvellous and ended up by singing."[1] The feeling was mutual. In 1972 Ethel wrote the following: "down through the years until he died [in 1964], we had this sincere and wonderful friendship. . . . More than once—many times—he'd give splendid affairs at his home with so many famous people it would make your head swim. And Carl would invite them to come this way: 'I want you to meet Miss Ethel Waters.' I was neither a VIP, nor was I on Skid Row. I was—Ethel Waters, the young woman this fine, great hearted man wanted them all to know."[2]

In 1951 Ethel's critically acclaimed and best-selling autobiography, *His Eye Is on the Sparrow*, coauthored with journalist Charles Samuels (who interviewed her almost daily for four months), was published, and in 1953 she made her final appearance on the Broadway stage. Ethel's one-woman show, *At Home with Ethel Waters*, opened at the 48th Street Theatre on September 22 and closed on October 10. Accompanied by Reginald Beane at the piano, Ethel sang many of the songs associated with her, and she received glowing reviews from the critics:

> Informality and effortlessness are the key to her performance from the moment she makes her first appearance in the single, attractive living room setting carrying a bouquet of flowers and seemingly going into her act more or less as an

afterthought. Most of the songs which have been associated with her long career are included. These are as rewarding as ever, but then so are some of the lesser known numbers—"I Ain't Gonna Sin No More," "Throw Dirt" and "Go Back Where You Stayed Last Night," for example. Each of these has in common an earthiness and ribaldry which have nothing in common with prurience; everything is frank and open. . . . Of course, all the songs are deeply indebted to her delivery of them. Miss Waters is such a perceptive actress that she can transform a mood from that of a benevolent mammy to that of a worldly-wise woman schooled in the devious ways of love, all with a slyly insinuating flicker of her remarkably expressive features, a roguish glint in her eye or a subtle twist of the hip. . . . All of this comes as naturally to her as the moving spirituals "Motherless Chile" and "Crucifixion."[3]

After appearing in *At Home with Ethel Waters*, there should have been greater challenges and successes awaiting Ethel, but instead there was a sharp decline in her fortunes. Her career practically ground to a halt. There were occasional television offers and summer stock revivals of *Member*, but mostly her public appearances were unhappy affairs. In 1955 she found herself heavily in debt. The Internal Revenue Service (IRS) hounded her for back taxes and seized the royalties on her autobiography. Ethel hit back at the IRS, announcing that she had worked only nine weeks in 1955. By this time, Ethel was not just unemployed, she was broke. In desperation, to help raise funds to pay off her debts, she made a television appearance on NBC's popular quiz show *Break the $250,000 Bank*, answering questions about music. "The appearance must have been humiliating," states Donald Bogle. "But it became part of a national spectacle as viewers tuned in to see if the fallen star would be able to get back on her feet. Somehow she managed to maintain her dignity and come through the quiz show experience with her self-respect intact. Waters won $10,000 on the program."[4]

Le Ruban Bleu (The Blue Ribbon) was one of the top nightclubs in New York in the late 1930s and 1940s. By the mid-1950s it was in decline. A few months after Ethel's appearance at the club, it was demolished. Says James Gavin:

The big surprise was an appearance in November 1956 by Ethel Waters, whom theatre and movies had long forgotten. She accepted this booking and another at the Bon Soir because she was broke. By now Waters had found God and sang mostly spirituals and gospel numbers—a disappointment to those hoping to hear "Am I Blue?" or "Happiness is a Thing Called Joe." Tired, immensely overweight, and frail of voice, Waters was no happier with the engagement, which she considered a humiliation. Recalls Bibi Osterwald, "She would come out and do her heavenly blessing, then go over to the cash register and say, 'Where the fuck is my money?'"[5]

The lowest point of all came when she appeared in a low-budget movie called *Carib Gold* (1956). Shot on location in Key West, Florida, local shrimp fishing fleets provided the background for a flimsy story about a sunken Spanish galleon laden with gold. Shot in an amateurish, documentary style, Ethel was billed solo, above the title, and played Mrs. Ryan (Mom), who runs a bar on the waterfront. Her son was played by Coley Wallace, who in real life, as a boxer, had fought—and beaten—future heavyweight champion Rocky Marciano when they were both amateurs. In 1953 Wallace played boxing champion Joe Louis in *The Joe Louis Story*, but though talented in the ring, he was no actor. In his second film, *Carib Gold*, he looks uncomfortable and stumbles over his lines. Ethel looks on in despair. She is given one song to perform: the terrible title song. The dramatic highlight of *Carib Gold* is the legendary Ethel comforting a distraught widow, played by a newcomer named Cicely Tyson. She would later inherit Ethel's crown as a movie earth mother with her monumental—and Oscar nominated—performance in *Sounder* (1972).

After the public humiliations of appearing on television's *Break the $250,000 Bank*, performing at Le Ruban Bleu, and starring in the film *Carib Gold*, it is hardly surprising Ethel dedicated her life to Jesus in 1957 and joined Billy Graham's crusades. In the mid- and late twentieth century, the Reverend Billy Graham played a significant part in the growth of evangelical Christianity in the United States and in the world. His "crusades" attracted huge gatherings of believing Christians, drawing thousands to hear his message, as millions more audience members participated through the medium of television. Ethel had grown tired of long periods of unemployment and taking job offers that were unworthy of her. The American entertainment world had turned its back on her when it should have been keeping her employed and celebrating her long and successful career.

It happened like this. Ethel was a guest on Tex McCrary's radio show when McCrary asked her if Billy Graham's forthcoming event at Madison Square Garden was going to be a success. Taken by surprise, Ethel replied: "God don't sponsor no flops!" After the show, which had been heard by a member of Graham's staff, Ethel was offered tickets to the crusade. She had sung at show business benefits at Madison Square Garden on many occasions through the years, but she said the night she attended the Graham crusade, "I was amazed at the serenity and the peace that pervaded. I sat there and I was so relaxed. What Billy said seemed like he was answering every question I had in my mind. Above all he kept saying how close the Lord is and I kept thinking God isn't far away, it was me shutting him out."[6]

Ethel had been listening to Billy Graham on the radio years before he appeared at Madison Square Garden. "He was a preacher that didn't use a whole gang of amen's and hallelujah's and he spoke in a language that my intellect could comprehend. I knew a lot about the saviour, and I knew religious talk. I wasn't a Bible-reading person but he clarified things in the modern day language vernacular. I had been listening to him, and following him down the years, but I was slightly annoyed when I saw him coming out from Minneapolis and saw that he was young and he was white [Ethel laughs]. The one thing I love about Billy, he glorifies Jesus. You know God used to go through so many of these places on stilts, and Jesus was taboo. I get so tired of hearing about the Holy Spirit and God, but Jesus is the one who paid the price. And I just loved Billy for that."[7]

From May 15 to September 1, 1957, more than two million went to New York's Madison Square Garden to hear Graham. For sixteen weeks Ethel attended the crusade, and during that time she joined the choir: "Each night I'd go out and I would just feel 'This is great.' I enjoyed it so much and I slept better than I had in many years. It was just like walking on air because I felt I was getting back to my Lord. And each time I attended the crusade I was getting strength."[8] Eventually Ethel was invited to sing solo, and the song was "His Eye Is on the Sparrow." Cliff Barrows, who conducted the choir, later recalled: "One of the moving experiences of my life was leading her that first time in singing with the choir, 'His Eye Is on the Sparrow.' She did it so beautifully, and seemed so obviously moved in her own heart and spirit, and I felt that the entire choir along with all of us on the music staff were caught up in it."[9] A black and white kinescope film, featuring Ethel singing "Sparrow" at Madison Square Garden on August 3, 1957, has survived. Ethel also acted in a film for Billy Graham's World Wide Pictures: *The Heart Is a Rebel* (1958). She played a kindhearted nurse who takes care of a sick child who has been rejected by his father.

Ethel was always religious, saying she thanked Jesus before she went on the stage to give a performance, but she didn't completely relinquish the stage to Him until 1957: "I don't care who you are, you can't serve two masters, and the stage don't fit in. And the stage was my livelihood. But Lord has He made me rich since then. I'm not talking about financial. I have everything I need and I feel secure. I have found in Him everything I need as I never had that shoulder or that lap, but I have it now in my spiritual strength and faith in Him."[10]

Ethel's involvement with Billy Graham not only removed her from the world of show business, it set her apart from the majority of African Americans. This happened in the 1950s and 1960s, when most African Americans, including show business personalities, were embracing and supporting civil rights. They were also finding inspiration in black leaders and political activists such as Martin Luther King, Malcolm X, Eldridge Cleaver, Angela Davis, Lorraine Hansberry, and James Baldwin. The slogan of the day was "Black is beautiful," but Ethel was having none of it. She upset civil rights organizations by proclaiming, "I'm only concerned with God-given rights, and they are available to everyone!" She came from a generation that used *black* as a term of abuse, and she rejected its new meaning. And yet, in 1951, Ethel had made her feelings clear on the matter of race pride in her autobiography. Even if she did not want to join marches, she was proud to be black: "I have the soundest of reasons for being proud of my people. We Negroes have always had such a tough time that our very survival in this white world with the dice always loaded against us is the greatest possible testimonial to our strength, our courage, and immunity to adversity."[11] Edward Mapp comments:

> People have a problem with in-your-face religion. Billy Graham has his supporters, but a vast majority of people don't really want that. Billy Graham's followers were mostly white and African Americans were uncomfortable seeing Ethel with them, even though she was singing spirituals. Now all this happened pre-Oprah Winfrey. Today, Oprah's appeal is mostly to whites and yet it is acceptable to African Americans. Ethel removed herself from the mainstream of performing and people were uncomfortable with what she became, but I think it was circumstantial. I don't think Ethel consciously embraced Billy Graham over black religion. One should respect Ethel's choice, but people don't always do what is right. In the African American community we have criticised blacks who "sold out" or we felt were too friendly with whites. And black people like Ethel have always been charged with that without people knowing the true story. They just see what they wish to see.[12]

Hollywood hadn't completely given up on Ethel. In 1959 she accepted an offer from 20th Century Fox to play Dilsey in a screen version of William Faulkner's classic novel from 1929, *The Sound and the Fury*. Directed by Martin Ritt, this melodrama, set in the Deep South, starred Joanne Woodward as the childlike Quentin, who falls in love with an unscrupulous carnival artist and almost loses her meager inheritance. Film historian David Shipman describes the film as "weird": "It emerges as a mixture of Tennessee Williams and Emily Bronte; if Margaret Leighton is splendid as a Blanche du Bois type, Yul Brynner is absurd as a Heathcliff figure."[13] Ethel was cast as the wise but long-suffering cook and servant Dilsey. The fourth section of the novel is sometimes known as "Dilsey's section" because she figures so prominently in it, but her role in the film version is diminished. It was generally agreed that Ethel, in her movie swan song, was wasted in an underwritten role.

Regrettably, Ethel was not offered what could have been her greatest role: the matriarch Lena Younger in Lorraine Hansberry's Broadway play *A Raisin in the Sun*. Hansberry won the New York Drama Critics Circle Award as best play of 1959 for her exploration of the trials and tribulations of an indestructible black family who live in a claustrophobic apartment in Chicago. A crisis looms when they are faced with an opportunity to integrate into a lily-white suburb. In the Broadway production—and subsequent film produced in 1961—a quartet of African American acting giants garnered rave reviews for their depiction of Hansberry's Younger family: Sidney Poitier (as Lena's son Walter Lee), Ruby Dee (as her daughter-in-law Ruth), Diana Sands (as her daughter Beneatha), and Claudia McNeil as Lena. In his autobiography *You Can't Do That on Broadway!* the play's producer Philip Rose recalls that Ethel was the obvious choice for the role of Lena: "We needed an actress in the appropriate age range and with the look and the power to play against Sidney Poitier. . . . She was very much considered in our discussions, but Lorraine and I felt strongly that we would be adding another easy choice for the audience to love and thereby do a disservice to the play." Ethel's name resurfaced in further casting discussions when it was felt that, from a commercial point of view, her name would attract audiences to the box office. The producer, Kermit Bloomgarden, told Rose: "The role of Mama requires a star, and we need someone to co-star with Mr. Poitier, who is not yet a star stage attraction. I have investigated, and know that I can get Ethel Waters to play that role and we'd be guaranteed a hit show." Rose acknowledged that Ethel was a fine actress and a great star, and an obvious choice for "Mama" Younger: "But since the beginning, *Raisin*, particularly from Lorraine's point of view, needed protection from becoming a play about Mama rather than her son, Walter Lee. Casting Ethel Waters in the role would have compounded the problem, which was, to be sure, never entirely eliminated from the play."[14]

Ethel had starred in *The Member of the Wedding* in 1952, but black actresses had to wait almost ten years before Hollywood provided strong dramatic leading roles for them. Though Juanita Moore had registered as Annie Johnson opposite Lana Turner in Douglas Sirk's brilliant tearjerker *Imitation of Life* (1959), a performance that earned her an Oscar nomination for best supporting actress, it was the 1961 screen version of *Raisin* that put black women center stage in a Hollywood movie. Says Aram Goudsouzian in his biography of Sidney Poitier: "The female characters stepped outside the boxes in which Hollywood placed black women. *A Raisin in the Sun* shattered stereotypes . . . and on a large scale."[15]

It is heartbreaking that Ethel was denied the opportunity to be part of the success of *A Raisin in the Sun* on stage and screen. The Broadway production earned Poitier and McNeil Tony nominations and ran for 530 performances. It would have been the crowning achievement of Ethel's career. Edward Mapp comments: "Ethel was so multi-dimensional and I often thought about why she did not play the role of the matriarch Lena Younger in *A Raisin in the Sun*. What a part! Ethel would have been wonderful, acting Lorraine Hansberry's lines."[16]

In 1966 Ethel traveled to London for the first time since 1930 to appear with Billy Graham in his month-long crusade. At Wembley Stadium the crusade attracted Britain's biggest-ever religious gathering, and extra police were brought in to control the crowd of 75,000. A 3,000-strong choir from London suburban churches sang well-known hymns, and Ethel sang spirituals. John Culme was in the audience:

> I went along rather reluctantly with a coach party from my mother's local church, just to see what Graham was like in the flesh, so to speak. Even then I was not impressed by religious matters so I was there in the guise of an observer only. To say that I was shocked by the sheer numbers there is an understatement. I was also shocked by the theatricality of the event, even down to Mr. Graham's manipulation of a silver-edged bible he held up in his hands while speaking, which nicely caught the floodlights, giving the impression that the book was burning in his hands. Wembley then was an oblong arena and he was on a raised dais on one of the sides, below the crowd; our seats were more or less opposite which gave us a good view but because of the distance he and his people appeared very small and far away. The "warm-up" consisted of a group of vocalists singing, as I recall, old negro spirituals. The lead singer was a very small old lady with iron grey hair, holding a microphone and fairly belting out the songs with a wonderful control and a familiar voice. I was captivated. Who on earth was this amazing woman? I strained to see but couldn't really distinguish her face, but it slowly dawned on me who she was. . . . I thought it was Miss Waters (I was certainly familiar with many of her old recordings then) but I had to consult the programme which one of our group had picked up on the way in. Frankly, I was as stunned as I was delighted. The Billy Graham event to me was nothing compared with this chance encounter with such a legend. I was thrilled and it remains to this day one of the highlights of my life as a lover of celebrities of the early 20th Century.[17]

In 1972 Ethel published *To Me It's Wonderful*—her "spiritual autobiography"—in which she tells how she found again the love of Jesus she had lost as a child. She also received occasional honors (see appendix A for a complete list). Ethel Waters Week was observed in her birthplace, Chester, Pennsylvania, from April 24 to 30, 1972, and she was present for the dedication of Ethel Waters Park at Third and Dock Streets, named in her honor. April 30, 1972, was proclaimed Ethel Waters Day in Philadelphia by then governor Milton Shapp. On October 6, 1972, Billy Graham honored Ethel with a testimonial dinner at the Century Plaza Hotel in Los Angeles. She was reunited with many friends, including Julie Harris, and guest speaker, Bob Hope, quipped, "She has brought more happiness to people than tax refunds." He added: "You have had your share of 'Stormy Weather' and have weathered many 'Heat Waves!' I hope you can walk in many green pastures before you reach your 'Cabin in the Sky.'" In 1974 Ethel was inducted into the American Theatre Hall of Fame, and in 1976 she was inducted into the Black Filmmakers Hall of Fame. On being asked how it felt to be a legend, Ethel replied:

That's what they say. I don't say that. I just say I've been wonderfully blessed from my first attempt at appearing in front of the public. I never wanted to go on the stage. I admired show people. I loved them from afar. I always did. And I love talent. None exists around today that's not in a wheelchair or walking with a cane. But I love artistry. . . . people always saw in me something I didn't see in myself. I never could do things that I couldn't identify with. No use nobody trying to tell me how to be a ballet dancer. But you could tell me how to shimmy because I got a butt and I knew then how to use it! [Ethel laughs.][18]

In 1976 a frail but still hearty Ethel made her last public appearance at the premiere of *That's Entertainment! Part 2* and, to promote the film, on Mike Douglas's television talk show (see chapter 10). For years Ethel had suffered ill health, and after being diagnosed with cancer of the uterus, by Christmas 1976 she was living in the home of her friends Juliann and Paul DeKorte. Paul, a musician, had traveled with Ethel on the Billy Graham crusades. Juliann, a registered nurse, movingly describes the final year of Ethel's life in *Finally Home*, published in 1978. Of Ethel's complex personality, Juliann notes:

I had given up long ago trying to understand Ethel Waters. She was completely unpredictable! I learned quickly to love and respect her with the awe that her very presence demanded, while developing a healthy fear of displeasing her. She could be stern and stubborn—yet gentle, loving, and kind. She could be blunt, unyielding, and strict—yet wise, generous, and forgiving. She even became frustrated at times with her own multi-faceted personality. She once admitted, "I'm more comfortable with Ethel Waters, now that she's a Christian. But I don't understand her all the time.". . . When she loved, she loved deeply. When she was hurt, the bitterness ate away like acid, until the Lord Jesus Christ came into her life and took it away. He became the Partner and Companion she had longed for and sought after for so many lonely years.[19]

Though her health deteriorated throughout 1977, Ethel never lost her sense of humor. Juliann recalls: "I learned to laugh with her when, because of her eyesight, she missed the glass while pouring water. I learned to chuckle with her about how her shoes had shrunk when her feet were too swollen to fit them for a trip to the doctor. She taught me that to laugh is better than to cry."[20] At this time, when Ethel was asked what brought her the greatest joy, she quickly responded: "When I can talk about the Lord. That's my greatest joy. And the security to know that when I have my tough moments I can call on Him. I might be found dead in here but I don't care nothing about it because He knows when he's gonna snap the lock on the suitcase!" Ethel passed away on September 1, 1977.

Ethel was not completely forgotten when her funeral took place at the Forest Lawn Memorial Park in Glendale, Los Angeles, California, on September 6. Flowers were sent from Sammy Davis Jr., Irving Berlin, MGM Studios, and Billy Graham (who was out of the country). Friends who attended included many she had made during her Billy Graham years, as well as show business pals, such as Pearl Bailey, John Bubbles, and Reginald Beane, her devoted accompanist for more than forty years. Two of her favorite songs were performed—"Just a Closer Walk with Thee" and "What a Friend We Have in Jesus"—and a tape recording of her singing "His Eye Is on the Sparrow" was played. At her graveside, Reginald Beane concluded the eulogies by sharing memories with the congregation about "LaBelle," his nickname for Ethel. He then read a poem they had both loved. Her memorial reads, simply, *Ethel Waters, His Eye Is on the Sparrow, 1896–1977.*

Notes

1. Bruce Kellner, ed. *Letters of Carl Van Vechten* (New Haven: Yale University Press, 1987), 242.

2. Ethel Waters, *To Me It's Wonderful* (New York: Harper and Row, 1972), 57–58.

3. Unidentified reviewer, *Theatre Arts*, November 1953, 23.

4. Donald Bogle, *Primetime Blues: African Americans on Network Television* (New York: Farrar, Straus and Giroux, 2001), 73.

5. James Gavin, *Intimate Nights: The Golden Age of New York Cabaret* (New York: Grove Weidenfeld, 1991), 146.

6. *Just a Little Talk with Ethel*, a two-LP set released on the World Records label in 1977.

7. *Just a Little Talk with Ethel.*

8. *Just a Little Talk with Ethel.*

9. Cliff Barrows, quoted in Twila Knaack, *Ethel Waters: I Touched a Sparrow* (Waco, Texas: Word Books, 1978), 43.

10. *Just a Little Talk with Ethel.*

11. Ethel Waters with Charles Samuels, *His Eye Is on the Sparrow* (New York: Da Capo, 1992), 93.

12. Edward Mapp, interview with Stephen Bourne, London, August 15, 2005.

13. David Shipman, *The Story of Cinema* (New York: St. Martin's Press, 1982), 1175.

14. Philip Rose, *You Can't Do That on Broadway!* (New York: Limelight, 2001), 81, 92.

15. Aram Goudsouzian, *Sidney Poitier: Man, Actor, Icon* (Chapel Hill: University of North Carolina Press, 2004), 186.

16. Mapp interview

17. John Culme, by e-mail, September 5, 2006. Reproduced with permission.

18. *Just a Little Talk with Ethel.*

19. Juliann DeKorte, *Finally Home* (Old Tappan, N.J.: Revell, 1978), 59–61.

20. DeKorte, *Finally Home*, 109.

APPENDIX A

~

Ethel Waters's Credits

Broadway Theatre

Africana (Daly's 63rd Street Theatre, July 11, 1927, to August 16, 1927. Transferred to National Theatre, August 20, 1927, to September 10, 1927, 72 performances). Revue. With Louis Douglas. EW performed "My Special Friend Is in Town," "Shake That Thing," "Dinah," "Take Your Black Bottom Outside," and "I'm Coming Virginia."

Lew Leslie's Blackbirds (aka *Blackbirds of 1930*) (Royale Theatre, October 22, 1930, to December, 1930, 57 performances). Revue. With Berry Brothers, Buck and Bubbles, Minto Cato, Broadway Jones, Cecil Mack's Choir, Flournoy Miller, Mantan Moreland, and Jazzlips Richardson. EW performed "You're Lucky to Me" and "My Handy Man Ain't Handy No More."

Rhapsody in Black (Sam H. Harris Theatre, May 4, 1931, to July 1931, 80 performances). Revue. With Valaida Snow, Berry Brothers, Earl (Snakehips) Tucker, and Cecil Mack Choir. EW performed "Washtub Rhapsody (Rubsody)," "Dancehall Hostess," "What's Keeping My Prince Charming?" and "You Can't Stop Me from Loving You."

As Thousands Cheer (Music Box Theatre, September 30, 1933, to September 8, 1934, 400 performances). Revue. With Helen Broderick, Marilyn Miller, and Clifton Webb. EW performed "Heat Wave," "Harlem on My Mind," "To Be or Not to Be," and "Supper Time."

At Home Abroad (Winter Garden Theatre, September 19, 1935, to January 1936. Transferred to Majestic Theatre, January 20, 1936, to March 7, 1936, 198 performances). Revue. With Beatrice Lillie and Eleanor Powell. EW performed "Hottentot Potentate," "Thief in the Night," "The Steamboard Whistle," and "Got a Bran' New Suit."

Mamba's Daughters (Empire Theatre, January 3, 1939, to May 20, 1939, 162 performances). Drama. With Reginald Beane, Anne Brown, Willie Bryant, Georgia Burke, Georgette Harvey, Alberta Hunter, Canada Lee, Maud Russell, and Fredi Washington. EW as Hagar.

Mamba's Daughters (Broadway Theatre, March 23, 1940, to April 6, 1940, 17 performances). Drama. For cast, see previous entry.

Cabin in the Sky (Martin Beck Theatre, October 25, 1940, to March 8, 1941, 156 performances). With Georgia Burke, Todd Duncan, Katherine Dunham, Rex Ingram, and Dooley Wilson. EW as Petunia Jackson performed "Taking a Chance on Love," "Cabin in the Sky," "Honey in the Honeycomb," and "Love Turned the Light Out."

Laugh Time (Shubert Theatre, September 8, 1943, to October 16, 1943. Transferred to Ambassador Theatre, October 17, 1943, to November 20, 1943, 126 performances). Revue. With Buck and Bubbles, Frank Fay, and Bert Wheeler.

Blue Holiday (Belasco Theatre, May 21, 1945, to May 26, 1945, 8 performances). Revue. With the Katherine Dunham Dancers (including Eartha Kitt), Josephine Premice, and Josh White.

The Member of the Wedding (Empire Theatre, January 5, 1950, to March 17, 1951, 501 performances). Drama. With Julie Harris and Brandon de Wilde. EW as Berenice Sadie Brown.

At Home with Ethel Waters (48th Street Theatre, September 22, 1953, to October 10, 1953, 23 performances). One-woman show. With Reginald Beane.

Off-Broadway

An Evening with Ethel Waters (Renata Theatre, from April 8, 1959). One-woman show. With Reginald Beane.

Author's note: On November 20, 1938, Ethel made an appearance at Carnegie Hall accompanied by the orchestra of Leonard de Paur. In 1945 she appeared in a summer stock production of The Voice of Strangers, *and in 1954 she had an unsuccessful pre-Broadway tryout of* Gentle Folk.

Film

On with the Show! (Warner Bros., 1929). Directed by Alan Crosland. EW as herself sings "Am I Blue?" and "Birmingham Bertha."

Rufus Jones for President (Vitaphone, 1933). Directed by Roy Mack. With Sammy Davis Jr. and Hamtree Harrington. EW sings "Stay on Your Side of the Fence," "Am I Blue?" and "Underneath a Harlem Moon."

Bubbling Over (RKO Radio, 1934). Directed by Leigh Jason. With Hamtree Harrington. EW sings "Darkies Never Dream" and "Taking Your Time."

Gift of Gab (Universal, 1934). Directed by Karl Freund. EW as herself sings "I Ain't Gonna Sin No More."

Tales of Manhattan (20th Century Fox, 1942). Directed by Julien Duvivier. With Paul Robeson and Eddie "Rochester" Anderson. EW as Hester sings "Glory Day" with Paul Robeson and chorus.

Cairo (MGM, 1942). Directed by Major W. S. Van Dyke II. With Jeanette MacDonald, Robert Young, and Dooley Wilson. EW as Cleona Jones sings "Buds Won't Bud."

Cabin in the Sky (MGM, 1943). Directed by Vincente Minnelli. With Eddie "Rochester" Anderson, Lena Horne, Rex Ingram, Butterfly McQueen, Louis Armstrong, and Duke Ellington. EW as Petunia Jackson sings "Happiness Is a Thing Called Joe," "Taking a Chance on Love," "Cabin in the Sky," and "Honey in the Honeycomb."

Stage Door Canteen (United Artists, 1943). Directed by Frank Borzage. EW as herself sings "Quicksand."

Pinky (20th Century Fox, 1949). Directed by Elia Kazan. With Jeanne Crain, Ethel Barrymore, William Lundigan, Frederick O'Neal, and Nina Mae McKinney. EW as Mrs. Dicey Johnson.

The Member of the Wedding (Columbia, 1952). Directed by Fred Zinnemann. With Julie Harris and Brandon de Wilde. EW as Berenice Sadie Brown sings "His Eye Is on the Sparrow."

Carib Gold (Splendora Film Corporation, 1956). Directed by Harold Young. With Coley Wallace. EW as Mrs. Ryan (Mom) sings "Carib Gold."

The Heart Is a Rebel (World Wide Pictures, 1958). Directed by Dick Ross. With John Milford and Georgia Lee. EW as Gladys sings "The Crucifixion," "His Eye Is on the Sparrow," and "Sometimes I Feel like a Motherless Child."

The Sound and the Fury (20th Century Fox, 1959). Directed by Martin Ritt. With Yul Brynner, Joanne Woodward, Margaret Leighton, and Stuart Whitman. EW as Dilsey.

In 1937 Ethel was caricatured in *Swing Wedding/Minnie the Moocher's Wedding Day*, an eight-minute MGM color cartoon parodying black performers and their music—represented as a frog colony. Other stars included Cab Calloway, Bill Robinson, Fats Waller, Louis Armstrong, and the Mills Brothers. In 1942 a three-minute "soundie" version of the cartoon—also featuring Ethel—was shown under the title *Hot Frogs*. In 1943 Ethel was seen performing "Am I Blue?" from *On with the Show!* in Warner Bros.' *The Voice That Thrilled the World* (1943), directed by Jean Negulesco. This short (two-reel) documentary traced the history of sound in the movies. Ethel can be seen in two Fox Movietone News productions: *Lee Shubert Funeral in New York City* (December 28, 1953) and *Island in the Sun Premiere, New York* (June 18, 1957), with the film's director, Robert Rossen, Mrs. Harry Belafonte (Julie Robinson), Red Buttons, Paulette Goddard, Lucille Ball, and Sammy Davis Jr. A kinescope exists of her performing "His Eye Is on the Sparrow" with the crusade choir at Billy Graham's Madison Square Garden rally (August 3, 1957), and newsreel film featuring Ethel also exists of his rally at Wembley (United Kingdom) (July 2, 1966). Ethel can be seen performing "Taking a Chance on Love" from *Cabin in the Sky* in the compilation feature *That's Entertainment! Part 2* (1976).

Television

The Ethel Waters Show (experimental) (NBC, June 14, 1939)
Borden Theater ("Ethel's Cabin") (August 1947)
Toast of the Town (CBS, October 2, 1949)

Beulah (series) (ABC, 1950–1952)
Toast of the Town (CBS, October 8, 1950)
Showtime USA (ABC, November 5, 1950)
This Is Show Business (CBS, March 1951)
G. E. Guest House (CBS, July 1951)
Toast of the Town (CBS, 1952)
The Jackie Gleason Show (CBS, November 7, 1952)
American Inventory (NBC, November 1, 1953)
Person to Person (CBS, January 8, 1954)
Tex and Jinx' Show (NBC, 1954)
Favorite Playhouse ("Speaking to Hannah") (January 23, 1955)
Climax! ("The Dance") (CBS, June 30, 1955)
General Electric Theater ("Winner by Decision") (CBS, November 6, 1955)
Playwrights '56 ("The Sound and the Fury") (December 6, 1955)
Twilight Theater (ABC, 1956)
Break the $250,000 Bank (NBC, 1956)
Saturday Spectacular ("Manhattan Tower") (NBC, October 27, 1956)
Matinee Theater ("Sing for Me") (NBC, October 21, 1957)
The Ford Show Starring Tennessee Ernie Ford (NBC, 1957)
The Mike Wallace Interview (ABC, 1958)
Whirlybirds ("The Big Lie") (June 8, 1959)
Route 66 ("Good Night, Sweet Blues") (CBS, October 6, 1961)
The Great Adventure ("Go Down Moses") (CBS, November 1, 1963)
Vacation Playhouse ("You're Only Young Twice") (pilot) (CBS, July 3, 1967)
The Hollywood Palace (ABC, March 8, 1969)
Daniel Boone ("Mamma Cooper") (NBC, February 5, 1970)
The Barbara McNair Show (syndicated, 1970)
The Pearl Bailey Show (ABC, 1971)
Owen Marshall: Counselor at Law ("Run, Carol, Run") (ABC, January 20, 1972)
Johnny Carson Presents Sun City Scandals '72 (special) (NBC, March 13, 1972)
The David Frost Show (syndicated, May 2, 1972)
The Tonight Show Starring Johnny Carson (NBC, May 10, 1972)
The Tonight Show Starring Johnny Carson (NBC, October 27, 1972)
Soul Free (1974)
The Mike Douglas Show (*Mike in Hollywood*) (syndicated, February 16, 1976)

Ethel has been featured in several major American television documentary series including *Brown Sugar: Eighty Years of America's Black Female Superstars*
(1986), written by Donald Bogle, narrated by Billy Dee Williams; *Jazz* (2001),
directed by Ken Burns, narrated by Keith David; and *Broadway: The American*

Musical (2004), directed by Michael Kantor, narrated by Julie Andrews, and winner of the Emmy for outstanding nonfiction series. There has yet to be a documentary made about Ethel.

Radio

Vaudeville (BBC) (1930)
All Negro Hour Club (1930)
Rudy Vallee Show (1933)
Broadcast twice weekly over the NBC network (1933)
Hall of Fame (1935)
A Song of Thanksgiving (1935)
Several appearances on Ben Bernie's show (1936–1937)
Harlem Rhapsodies (1937)
CBS European broadcast from the Cotton Club (1937)
All-Colored Revue (1937)
Bing Crosby Show (1941)
Jubilee (1941)
Command Performance (1942)
Reader's Digest (1943)
The Man Who Went to War (BBC) (1944)
Amos 'n' Andy (1944)
The Big Show (1951)
Cavalcade of America (Sixteen Sticks in a Bundle) (1952)
Harlem Amateur Hour (1952)
Dwight Cooke's Guestbook (1953)
Make Up Your Mind (1954)

Discography

According to Ethel's second autobiography, *To Me It's Wonderful* (1972), after eight years of research, Mr. George Finola of New Orleans had compiled the only known complete discography of Ethel's recordings. The remarkable list totaled 259. Regrettably, only an abridged version appeared in the book. It was impossible to include a detailed discography in this publication, but since the 1990s, CD (compact disc) compilations have made it possible to listen to most of Ethel's recording output from the 1920s to the 1940s. Later recordings, including a live performance in 1957, with Reginald Beane on piano, and several religious albums, including *His Eye Is on the Sparrow* (1960) and *Just a Little Talk with Ethel* (1977), as well as a gospel EP recorded in 1966, have become collector's items. Among the best compilations on CD are the Classics Chronological Series, released from 1992 to 1994, which includes Ethel's complete recording output from 1921 to 1946; *Ethel Waters Featuring Benny Goodman and Duke Ellington 1929–1939* (Timeless, 1995), compiled by Chris Ellis, who also contributed the liner notes; *Cabin in the Sky* (Turner, 1996), which contains the original film soundtrack, with "outtakes," including a previously unissued duet between Ethel and Butterfly McQueen called "Dat Suits Me," and comprehensive liner notes by its coproducer, Marilee Bradford; *Ethel Waters: Am I Blue?* (Living Era, 1999); and *The Favourite Songs of Ethel Waters* (Sepia Records, 2006).

Awards and Tributes

Oscar nomination for best supporting actress (*Pinky*, 1949)

Plaque from the Negro Actors Guild (*Pinky*, 1949)

St. Genesius Medal from the American National Theatre Academy (1951)

Emmy nomination for outstanding single performance by a lead actress (*Route 66*, 1961–1962)

Park named in Ethel's honor in Chester, Pennsylvania (1972)

Inducted into American Theatre Hall of Fame (1974)

Inducted into Black Filmmakers Hall of Fame (1976)

Posthumously inducted into the Gospel Music Association's Gospel Music Hall of Fame (1984)

Ethel Waters: Stormy Weather at the National Film Theatre (London, December 7–28, 1993). Film retrospective compiled and presented by Stephen Bourne. Screenings included *On with the Show!*, *Bubbling Over*, *Cairo*, *Cabin in the Sky*, *Pinky*, *The Member of the Wedding*, and *The Sound and the Fury*.

Ethel's likeness appears on a United States postage stamp (1994)

Ethel's 1925 recording of "Dinah" inducted into the Grammy Hall of Fame in the category of Traditional Pop (Single) (1998)

Ethel's 1933 recording of "Stormy Weather" inducted into the Grammy Hall of Fame in the category of Jazz (Single) (2003)

Author's note: At the time of writing, Ethel has not been honored with a Grammy Lifetime Achievement Award, though numerous singers she influenced have been recognized, some of them posthumously. These include Ella Fitzgerald (1967), Mahalia Jackson (1972), Billie Holiday (1987), Lena Horne (1989), and Sarah Vaughan (1989). Other African American women who have been acknowledged include Marian Anderson (1991), Etta James (2003), and Jessye Norman (2006). Ethel is also waiting for a star bearing her name to be included among the 2,500 names honored on Hollywood's Walk of Fame.

There have been several attempts to dramatize Ethel's life. In 1978 Charles Fuller's Sparrow in Flight *opened off-Broadway, starring Ethel Ayler. Fuller, an African American playwright, is best known for* A Soldier's Play, *winner of the 1982 Pulitzer Prize and filmed as* A Soldier's Story *in 1984. A musical retrospective called* Miss Waters, to You *was produced by the AMAS Repertory Theatre, New York, in 1983. Based on a concept by Rosetta LeNoire, it featured music from Ethel's repertoire. In 2005 Larry Parr's one-woman play with music,* His Eye Is on the Sparrow, *opened at the Florida Studio Theatre. Jannie Jones and Chaundra Cameron alternated the role of Ethel.*

In 1979 Diahann Carroll paid tribute to Ethel in Black Broadway, *a concert at New York's Avery Fisher Hall featuring a host of veteran black musical performers, including Honi Coles, Adelaide Hall, Eubie Blake, Edith Wilson, and Herb Jeffries. Diahann included "Am I Blue?" "Taking a Chance on Love," "Happiness Is a Thing Called Joe," "Dinah," and "Stormy Weather" in her repertoire. Subsequently, Diahann recorded a tribute to Ethel with the Duke Ellington Orchestra.*

APPENDIX B

~

Transcript of BBC Radio 4's
Woman's Hour Interview

In Britain there have been several BBC radio tributes to Ethel. These include *Spotlight On . . . Ethel Waters* (BBC Radio 2, January 7, 1992) and *Voices* (BBC Radio 2, August 22, 1994). The following is a transcript of an interview broadcast in *Woman's Hour* on BBC Radio 4, December 9, 1993, to coincide with the film tribute to Ethel at the National Film Theatre in London (see the introduction). The participants are Jenni Murray (interviewer), Stephen Bourne (who was responsible for programming the film tribute), and actress and singer Joanne Campbell, who had portrayed a character based on Ethel in the musical *The Cotton Club*. This opened in London's West End at the Aldwych Theatre on January 24, 1992. Joanne had also portrayed Josephine Baker in *This Is My Dream* at the Theatre Royal, Stratford East, in 1986.

Ethel sings "Stormy Weather."

JENNI: It was written for her and she was the first to perform it live on the stage of the Cotton Club sixty years ago. Ethel Waters was one of the most influential black performers of the twenties, thirties, and forties. She appeared in films like *Cabin in the Sky* and *The Sound and the Fury* and was nominated for an Oscar for her role in *Pinky*. Well, this month there's a season of films at the National Film Theatre to celebrate the life of a forgotten pioneer. Joanne Campbell is an actress and singer who appeared as Millie Gibson, the Ethel Waters figure, in the musical *The Cotton Club*.

Stephen Bourne has put together the program for the NFT. Stephen, I think "Stormy Weather" is now very much associated with Lena Horne, with Ella Fitzgerald. Ethel Waters said it was the story of her life. Why?

STEPHEN: Ethel had a very troubled life. Her beginnings were particularly traumatic. She was conceived when her mother was raped at knifepoint, and Ethel then had a very dramatic childhood when she was a runner for pimps and prostitutes. She struggled out of that into black vaudeville and from there went into the Cotton Club, Broadway, and Hollywood. But it was a constant battle all the time.

JENNI: So how did she come to sing this song? It's now such a twentieth-century classic.

STEPHEN: She was a headliner at the Cotton Club, and Ted Koehler and Harold Arlen wrote this song especially for her, and she felt that the lyrics portrayed her life beautifully. It just encapsulated everything she'd experienced.

JENNI: Now Joanne, you did a lot of work on the Cotton Club for your appearance in the musical. How segregated were black artists from the mainstream in the time that she was performing?

JOANNE: Oh, very segregated. I mean if we look back into the twenties and thirties we could say that America was under apartheid in a similar way we now see with South Africa, and what was so unique about the Cotton Club was that, although there were a lot of black artists and also black staff at the front of house, serving and performing at the club, they were never allowed to mix socially with the white Americans. It was a microcosm of the whole system of America at that time.

JENNI: Now your Millie Gibson was based on Ethel. What was so special about her compared to her contemporaries? Like Bessie Smith, like Ma Rainey?

JOANNE: Well, as Stephen has said, Ethel had a way of performing her songs that carried them beyond just being a singer, doing a blues number. She would put a lot of drama into the numbers, so in fact each one became a little vignette. She always tried to make sure that her songs would communicate to her audience that she was letting them into the life of a black woman in America. And it was particularly poignant in the Cotton Club because it was considered the place by the white socialites as somewhere where you could forget your troubles and be exposed to the heady frivolous energy of black jazz. But Ethel would always find a way of encompassing the true life of black entertainers in her music. So by speaking of her own personal experience, she was also enlightening them about what other things were happening for black people in the country.

JENNI: She was a bit of a battler wasn't she? She had a do with Bessie Smith.

STEPHEN: She did at the beginning of her career in black vaudeville. But there was a lot of competitiveness because there were so few opportunities for black women to perform, and Bessie didn't think very highly of Ethel when Ethel decided to sing one of her numbers, "St. Louis Blues," on the same stage, in the same show. There was some conflict there.

JENNI: How did she break into Hollywood films?

STEPHEN: She came into films early as a guest star, but later her Broadway hit *Cabin in the Sky* was picked up by MGM, and they asked her to come out to Hollywood to take the leading role, which she had played on Broadway.

JENNI: Stephen, how did she make parts like these her own, because often parts written for her type of actress were really rather crude stereotypes, and she totally transcended that.

STEPHEN: She did. In fact, to be fair, a lot of the black American actresses did in their own way, and Ethel certainly brought great warmth and humanity to these roles. It was quite remarkable what she was able to do.

JENNI: Why do you think she found it easier to switch to film work and acting than perhaps her contemporaries did?

JOANNE: I think from early on really she always had an integrity that transcended just being an entertainer. Unfortunately for a lot of black performers at the time, the hidden code for success was to always please, always be pleasant, always have an air that there weren't any problems. Because she was so immensely talented as a singer, because she didn't just sing blues— she was very good at doing her own renditions of popular white American jazz at the time—and because of that unique style of portrayal, it seemed quite feasible that she would become an actress.

JENNI: But what about the others? Bessie Smith, Ma Rainey? Surely they could have done it too?

JOANNE: It's very difficult to say, yes, they could have. One could take any group of singers and ask why one became an actress and another didn't. Each singer has a unique style, and hers is so special because of her emphasis on drama. It just seemed she would be the one to do that.

JENNI: Why has she become forgotten in recent years when the other names have stayed with us?

STEPHEN: My theory is that she became too big, too powerful, too threatening, and certainly her performance in *The Member of the Wedding* is very striking, and unnerving, because it's so real. And sadly she did go into decline, partly because of health problems, partly because while they were writing great parts for Ethel Barrymore when she was older, they wouldn't do that for Ethel Waters.

JENNI: What happened to her?

STEPHEN: She was always a religious woman, but she became very religious in the late 1950s when her career went into decline, and she joined Billy Graham and his crusades and spent the last twenty years of her life with them.

JOANNE: She was one of those artists who knew what she wanted, and from the beginning it was very clear to her what her objectives were as a performer. She had a message for mankind about the lives of black people, and unfortunately Hollywood producers didn't want that to come through. So, if one didn't keep quiet, you wouldn't get the work, and she suffered because of that.

JENNI: As a performer how important has she been for someone like you?

JOANNE: Very important really because what we see with someone like her is that if you have the courage to be truthful to where you come from, and your own experiences, and you do use that heavily to emphasise how you play a part, whether you're singing or acting, then you can only go from strength to strength as an artist.

JENNI: And has she influenced a line of women?

JOANNE: Oh, definitely. Unfortunately when people mention "Stormy Weather" they immediately think of Lena Horne. It's unbelievable. The song was written for Ethel.

Ethel sings "Am I Blue?"

JENNI: A stunning Ethel Waters, and my thanks to Stephen Bourne and Joanne Campbell.

APPENDIX C

~

Testimonials

The following collection of testimonials to Ethel spans more than sixty years, from 1942 to 2005. They summarize Ethel's importance as an influential, but neglected, singer. In spite of the comments made here, Ethel is still considered the poor relation of several jazz giants, including Ella Fitzgerald and Billie Holiday. As a popular black performer of the last century, she is not as well remembered or celebrated as some of her contemporaries. For example, Josephine Baker and Paul Robeson have been the subjects of many biographies and documentaries. No documentary has been made about Ethel, and until now, the only books written about her were published in 1978. As jazz authority Dan Morgenstern says, "She falls between the cracks."

Hugues Panassie in *The Real Jazz* (1942) (translated from French to English by Anne Sorelle Williams). Panassie was a French jazz critic who, during the Second World War, allegedly used jazz recordings as a way to defy Nazi authority in France:

> In addition to the blues singers, there are those who have not specialized in the blues but only sing them incidentally. Naturally their style is quite different. Without any question, the best seem to me to be Ethel Waters and Ella Fitzgerald. But Ethel Waters should not be judged by the commercial interpretations with which she has had increasing success during the years. However, in such records as "Shake That Thing" and "My Handy Man," she sings with complete sincerity. Here is the very opposite of Bessie Smith. Ethel Waters's voice has little volume and is pleasant but not at all harsh; she swings less from any dynamic

strength than from a delicate suppleness. Her singing is light, full of graceful in-flections, and is in no way affected. Moreover, her diction is excellent, and she sings with incomparable accuracy. Her range is extensive; she is at ease in the extremely high and low registers. Here you get a feeling of complete freedom and of a truly fine quality.

William Gardner Smith in *Phylon* (1950):

Was she the greatest? It is hard to say in a world filled with greats. But this much, surely, is certain: if she did not stand head and shoulders above every-one else, at least no one stood even an inch above her. She occupied the heights held by Calloway and Ellington and Robinson—so that a latter day bi-ographer of the Duke was led to remark that the downtown Cotton Club folded solely because it could not obtain enough acts of their calibre to keep the place going between engagements of these "titans." What was the secret of her success? Perhaps it was her warmth, her visible humanity. Audiences felt drawn to her, caught up by her, held by the personality which came through words and dance.

British jazz critic and journalist Chris Ellis in *Storyville* (1969):

It is the rhythmic subtlety and freedom of her phrasing that make a profound impact on today's listener. To put it in a nutshell—Ethel swings! She swings, what is more, in a manner that is ten years ahead of its time. Even Bessie Smith, herself, sounds stolid and heavy by comparison, at least until, in the twilight of her recording career. . . . This is no criticism of Bessie, rightly named Empress of the Blues. To clarify a little, no-one would claim that Bessie swings in the way that one would apply that word to Ella Fitzgerald, and indeed Ella's kind of swinging is regarded as dating from the 1930s. Yet this is precisely the way Ethel was swinging as far back as 1921. . . . Ethel Waters' style of singing led directly to Ella and from her to Sarah Vaughan and the entire school of cur-rent jazz singers. . . . But if anyone believes that she ever lost her ability to sing jazz, try the soundtrack version of "Taking a Chance on Love" from the film of *Cabin in the Sky* where she proves over several choruses that she could still swing up a storm. . . . I suspect that much of the criticism of Ethel Waters stems from the fact that her singing refuses to fit neatly into some pigeonhole la-belled jazz or blues, or for that matter pop. . . . For my money, Ethel Waters is not merely a jazz singer, but the very first jazz singer on record.

Ken Barnes in *Sinatra and the Great Song Stylists* (1972):

Ethel's was not the big deep-voiced blues shouting of Bessie Smith. Her voice, though basically contralto, was smaller and very much lighter and more agile, with a sweet rounded tone and a wide range, but her greatest gifts were her rhythmic sense and a way with a lyric which places her securely among the two or three best interpreters in the history of popular music. Ethel Waters is a great dramatic actress and this comes through when she sings a song. A classic performance such as she gave to Irving Berlin's Suppertime, with its sombre lyrics of lynching and heartbreak, can only be compared with the very best of Billie Holiday or Bessie Smith.

Henry Pleasants in *The Great American Popular Singers* (1974):

Along with Bessie Smith and Louis Armstrong, she was a fountainhead of all that is finest and most distinctive in American popular singing. Of the three, she may well have been the most widely and the most perceptively influential. Louis Armstrong's vocalism, if not his phrasing, has defied imitation. Bessie Smith's singing was too little touched by white example. Bessie's influence has come down to us through gospel song and the blues. In Ethel Waters one hears almost everybody. In just about every popular singer who came after her one hears a bit of Ethel Waters.

Linda Dahl in *Stormy Weather: The Music and Lives of a Century of Jazzwomen* (1984):

Most of the so-called blues singers of the twenties, trained in those pre-microphone days in vaudeville, tent shows, revues and so on, were quite precise in their stage diction and gave full value to their song lyrics. Perhaps the prime example is Ethel Waters, who sang blues material early in her career but developed into a sophisticated singer of popular song with a jazz approach. The style she had perfected by the thirties nicely illustrates the difference between straight and jazz-based pop singing. With a fairly direct reading of the lyric, she manipulated tone, timbre and rhythm to give her delivery a permeating jazz flavor. Unfamiliar with such techniques, straight pop singers of her era could not hope to equal the subtleness and suppleness of her sound. Later pop-jazz singers followed Waters' lead in the idiom, developing further subtleties in the manipulation of rhythm, phrasing, shading and emphasis.

Dan Morgenstern, international jazz authority and director of the Institute of Jazz Studies at Rutgers University since 1976, interviewed by Susannah McCorkle in "The Mother of Us All," *American Heritage* (1994):

Besides being important in her own right, she is the link between blues and jazz. She paid a lot of attention to Louis—everyone did—but then everyone paid a lot of attention to her. Billie took key songs from her repertoire, even took blues lyrics she had written and recorded them as "Billie's Blues." Lena is a carbon copy of Ethel; just listen to both their records of "Stormy Weather." Because everything is handed down. People do little independent listening any more; it's all received wisdom. She never made the list. She falls between the cracks; the cabaret world doesn't recognise her either.

Randall Cherry, "Ethel Waters: The Voice of an Era," in *Temples for Tomorrow: Looking Back at the Harlem Renaissance* (2001):

Perhaps it is precisely because her influence was so widespread that she has not gotten the attention she deserves. Waters's all-encompassing output—covering blues, jazz, and popular song—almost seems to defy a truly fair and comprehensive treatment. This in part explains why, more often than not, Waters is relegated to a gray area between the earlier generation of "classic" blues singers and more recent jazz vocalists such as Holiday, Vaughan, and Fitzgerald.

British journalist Zenga Longmore, who became a fan of Ethel's in the 1970s, recently posted this appraisal on the Internet (April 7, 2005):

My first encounter with the unique Ethel Waters shall shine forever in my memory. The year was 1975 and I was listening to a collection of old 1930s gramophone records. All of a sudden Ethel's opening bars of "Frankie and Johnny" [recorded in 1938] thrilled the air. I was riveted by the voice—by the plot. . . . Nearly seventy years later, Ethel retains the power to generate tears. Her talents defy categorisation. Blues, jazz, gospel, ballads, show tunes and even Hebraic chants were all a part of this extraordinary woman's repertoire. Her voice was indescribably rich with a remarkable range of over four octaves. One of the most disturbing mysteries of modern times is why the world has forgotten her. Why, one wonders, do certain entertainers "endure" and others, who were equally famous in their time and just as talented, become obsolete? Perhaps the critics are to blame. George Melly, who should have known better, once claimed that Bessie Smith was the world's finest blues singer, but that Ethel sounded too "white." Mr. Melly and his boorish gang of jazz buffs should realise that it is the white singers who sounded like Ethel, not the other way round. Sophie Tucker, billed as "The Last of the Red Hot Mamas," even paid La Waters for private performances so she could study Ethel's style of delivery. Judy Garland and Frank Sinatra both admitted to having been influenced by Ethel.

~

Bibliography

Albertson, Chris. *Bessie: Empress of the Blues*. London: Abacus, 1975.

Anderson, Jervis. *Harlem: The Great Black Way 1900–1950*. London: Orbis, 1982.

Aschenbrenner, Joyce. *Katherine Dunham: Dancing a Life*. Urbana: University of Illinois Press, 2002.

Baker, Jean-Claude, and Chris Chase. *Josephine: The Hungry Heart*. Holbrook, Mass.: Adams, 1993.

Baker, Josephine, and Jo Bouillon. *Josephine*. New York: Harper and Row, 1977.

Baldwin, James. *The Devil Finds Work*. London: Joseph, 1976.

Barnes, Ken. *Sinatra and the Great Song Stylists*. London: Allan, 1972.

Barrett, Mary Ellin. *Irving Berlin: A Daughter's Memoir*. London: Simon and Schuster, 1995.

Barrios, Richard. *A Song in the Dark: The Birth of the Musical Film*. New York: Oxford University Press, 1995.

Bauml Duberman, Martin. *Paul Robeson*. London: Bodley Head, 1989.

Beckford, Ruth. *Katherine Dunham: A Biography*. New York: Dekker, 1979.

Behlmer, Rudy, ed. *Memo from Darryl F. Zanuck: The Golden Years at Twentieth Century-Fox*. New York: Grove Press, 1993.

Bergreen, Laurence. *As Thousands Cheer: The Life of Irving Berlin*. London: Hodder and Stoughton, 1990.

Bogle, Donald. *Toms, Coons, Mulattoes, Mammies and Bucks: An Interpretive History of Blacks in American Films*. New York: Bantam, 1974.

———. *Brown Sugar: Eighty Years of America's Black Female Superstars*. New York: Harmony, 1980.

———. *Blacks in American Films and Television: An Illustrated Encyclopedia*. New York: Garland, 1988.

———. *Dorothy Dandridge: A Biography*. New York: Amistad, 1997.

——. *Prime Time Blues: African Americans on Network Television.* New York: Farrar, Straus and Giroux, 2001.

——. *Bright Boulevards, Bold Dreams: The Story of Black Hollywood.* New York: One World/Ballantine, 2005.

Bourne, Stephen. "Denying Her Place: Hattie McDaniel's Surprising Acts." In Pam Cook and Philip Dodd, eds., *Women and Film: A Sight and Sound Reader.* London: Scarlet Press, 1993.

——. "Weather Girl (Ethel Waters)." *The Wire* (December/January 1993–1994), 44–45.

——. "Ethel Waters." In Horace Newcomb, ed., *Encyclopedia of Television.* Vol. 3. Chicago: Fitzroy Dearborn, 1997.

——. *Black in the British Frame: The Black Experience in British Film and Television.* London: Continuum, 2001.

——. "Ethel Waters." In Robert Aldrich and Garry Wotherspoon, eds., *Who's Who in Gay and Lesbian History: From Antiquity to World War II.* London: Routledge, 2001.

——. *Sophisticated Lady: A Celebration of Adelaide Hall.* London: ECOHP, 2001.

——. *Elisabeth Welch: Soft Lights and Sweet Music.* Lanham, Md.: Scarecrow Press, 2005.

Bricktop with James Haskins. *Bricktop.* New York: Atheneum, 1983.

Bridson, D. G. *Prospero and Ariel: The Rise and Fall of Radio: A Personal Recollection.* London: Gollancz, 1971.

Brown, Sterling. *Negro Poetry and Drama and the Negro in American Fiction.* New York: Atheneum, 1969.

Bushell, Garvin, and Mark Tucker. *Jazz from the Beginning.* Oxford: Bayou Press, 1988.

Cameron Williams, Iain. *Underneath a Harlem Moon: The Harlem to Paris Years of Adelaide Hall.* London: Continuum, 2002.

Carley, Charles E. "Ethel Waters." *Classic Film Collector*, no. 42 (Spring 1974), 26–27.

Cherry, Randall. "Ethel Waters: The Voice of an Era." In Genevieve Fabre and Michel Feith, eds., *Temples for Tomorrow: Looking Back at the Harlem Renaissance.* Bloomington: Indiana University Press, 2001.

——. "Ethel Waters: Long, Lean, Lanky Mama." In Robert Springer, ed., *Nobody Knows Where the Blues Come From: Lyrics and History.* Jackson: University Press of Mississippi, 2005.

Chilton, John. *Who's Who in Jazz.* London: Bloomsbury, 1970.

Ciment, Michel. *Kazan on Kazan.* London: Secker and Warburg, 1973.

Clark Hine, Darlene, ed. *Facts on File Encyclopedia of Black Women in America: Theater Arts and Entertainment.* New York: Facts on File, 1997.

Cripps, Thomas. *Slow Fade to Black: The Negro in American Film 1900–1942.* London: Oxford University Press, 1977.

Crowther, Bruce, and Mike Pinfold. *The Jazz Singers: From Ragtime to the New Wave.* Poole, U.K.: Blandford Press, 1986.

Cullen, Frank. "Ethel Waters: The Mother of Us All." *Classic Images*, no. 253 (July 1996), 17–21.

Cunard, Nancy, ed. *Negro: An Anthology*. New York: Ungar, 1970.

Dahl, Linda. *Stormy Weather: The Music and Lives of a Century of Jazz Women*. London: Quartet, 1984.

———. *Morning Glory: A Biography of Mary Lou Williams*. Berkeley: University of California Press, 1999.

Deffaa, Chip. *Voices of the Jazz Age: Profiles of Eight Vintage Jazzmen*. Oxford: Bayou Press, 1990.

DeKorte, Juliann. *Ethel Waters: Finally Home*. Old Tappan, N.J.: Fleming, 1978.

Duval Harrison, Daphne. *Black Pearls: Blues Queens of the 1920s*. New Brunswick: Rutgers University Press, 1990.

Egan, Bill. *Florence Mills: Harlem Jazz Queen*. Lanham, Md.: Scarecrow Press, 2004.

Ellis, Chris. "Ethel Waters: Jazz Singer." *Storyville*, no. 22 (April/May 1969), 128–32.

———. Liner notes for CD compilation *Ethel Waters Featuring Benny Goodman and Duke Ellington 1929–1939*. Timeless Records, 1995.

Fordin, Hugh. *The World of Entertainment! Hollywood's Greatest Musicals*. New York: Doubleday, 1975.

Gardner Smith, William. "Phylon Profile, XXI: Ethel Waters." *Phylon* 11, no. 2 (1950), 114–20.

Gavin, James. *Intimate Nights: The Golden Age of New York Cabaret*. New York: Grove Weidenfeld, 1991.

Giddins, Gary. "The Mother of Us All." *Riding on a Blue Note: Jazz and American Pop*. New York: Oxford University Press, 1981.

Goode Robeson, Eslanda. *Paul Robeson: Negro*. London: Gollancz, 1930.

Gourse, Leslie, ed. *The Billie Holiday Companion: Seven Decades of Commentary*. London: Schirmer, 1997.

Green, Stanley. *The World of Musical Comedy*. South Brunswick, N.J.: Barnes, 1968.

———. *Encyclopedia of the Musical*. London: Cassell, 1976.

———. *Hollywood Musicals: Year by Year*. Milwaukee: Leonard, 1990.

———. *Broadway Musicals: Show by Show* (5th ed., revised and updated by Kay Green). Milwaukee: Leonard, 1996.

Gussow, Mel. *Darryl F. Zanuck: "Don't Say Yes Until I Finish Talking."* New York: Da Capo, 1980.

Harvey, Stephen. *Directed by Vincente Minnelli*. New York: Harper and Row, 1989.

Haskins, Jim. *The Cotton Club*. London: Robson, 1985.

Higham, Charles, and Joel Greenberg. *Hollywood in the Forties*. London: Zwemmer, 1968.

Holiday, Billie, with William Dufty. *Lady Sings the Blues*. New York: Doubleday, 1956.

Horne, Lena, with Richard Schickel. *Lena*. London: Deutsch, 1966.

Hughes, Langston. *The Big Sea: An Autobiography*. New York: Knopf, 1940.

Hughes, Langston, and Milton Meltzer. *Black Magic: A Pictorial History of the African-American in the Performing Arts*. Englewood Cliffs, N.J.: Prentice Hall, 1967.

Jablonski, Edward. *Harold Arlen: Happy with the Blues*. New York: Doubleday, 1961.

Jackson, Carlton. *Hattie: The Life of Hattie McDaniel.* London: Madison, 1990.

Johnson, James Weldon. *Black Manhattan.* New York: Knopf, 1930.

Jones, Christopher John. "Image and Ideology in Kazan's *Pinky.*" *Literature/Film Quarterly* 9, no. 2 (1981), 110–20.

Katz, Ephraim. *The Macmillan Film Encyclopedia* (4th ed.). London: Macmillan, 2001.

Kazan, Elia. *Elia Kazan: A Life.* London: Deutsch, 1988.

Kimball, Robert, and William Bolcom. *Reminiscing with Sissle and Blake.* New York: Viking, 1973.

Kisch, John, and Edward Mapp. *A Separate Cinema: Fifty Years of Black Cast Posters.* New York: Noonday Press, 1992.

Knaack, Twila. *Ethel Waters: I Touched a Sparrow.* Waco, Texas: Word, 1978.

Kreuger, Miles. Liner notes for LP *Ethel Waters on Stage and Screen 1925–1940.* Columbia Records, 1967.

Landay, Eileen. *Black Film Stars.* New York: Drake, 1973.

Larkin, Colin. *The Guinness Who's Who of Film Musicals.* London: Guinness, 1994.

———. *The Guinness Who's Who of Stage Musicals.* London: Guinness, 1994.

Levering Lewis, David. *When Harlem Was in Vogue.* New York: Knopf, 1981.

Lumet Buckley, Gail. *The Hornes: An American Family.* London: Weidenfeld and Nicholson, 1987.

MacDonald, J. Fred. *Blacks and White TV: Afro-Americans in Television since 1948.* Chicago: Nelson-Hall, 1983.

Mapp, Edward. *Blacks in American Films: Today and Yesterday.* Metuchen, N.J.: Scarecrow Press, 1972.

———. *Directory of Blacks in the Performing Arts* (2nd ed.). London: Scarecrow Press, 1990.

———. *African Americans and the Oscar: Seven Decades of Struggle and Achievement.* Lanham, Md.: Scarecrow Press, 2003.

Marks, Carole, and Diane Edkins. *The Power of Pride: Stylemakers and Rulebreakers of the Harlem Renaissance.* New York: Crown, 1999.

McCorkle, Susannah. "The Mother of Us All." *American Heritage* (February/March 1994), 61–73.

McCullers, Carson. *The Member of the Wedding.* Boston: Houghton Mifflin, 1946.

———. *The Member of the Wedding.* Play. New York: New Directions, 1951.

McVay, Douglas. *The Musical Film.* London: Zwemmer, 1967.

Meeker, David. *Jazz in the Movies.* London: Talisman, 1981.

Minnelli, Vincente, with Hector Arce. *I Remember It Well.* London: Angus and Robertson, 1975.

Naremore, James. *The Films of Vincente Minnelli.* Cambridge: Cambridge University Press, 1993.

Newcomb, Horace, ed. *Encyclopedia of Television.* Chicago: Fitzroy Dearborn, 1997.

Nicholson, Stuart. *A Portrait of Duke Ellington: Reminiscing in Tempo.* London: Sidgwick and Jackson, 1999.

Noble, Peter. *The Negro in Films.* London: Skelton Robinson, 1948.

O'Connor, Patrick, and Bryan Hammond. *Josephine Baker*. London: Cape, 1988.

Osborne, Robert. *Academy Awards Illustrated: A Complete History of Hollywood's Academy Awards in Words and Pictures*. La Habra, California: ESE, 1969.

Parish, James Robert, and Michael R. Pitts. *Hollywood Songsters: A Biographical Dictionary*. New York: Garland, 1991.

Pauly, Thomas H. *An American Odyssey: Elia Kazan and American Culture*. Philadelphia: Temple University Press, 1983.

Peary, Danny. *Alternate Oscars: One Critic's Defiant Choices for Best Picture, Actor, and Actress: From 1927 to the Present*. London: Simon and Schuster, 1993.

Placksin, Sally. *Jazzwomen 1900 to the Present: Their Words, Lives and Music*. London: Pluto Press, 1985.

Pleasants, Henry. *The Great American Popular Singers*. London: Gollancz, 1974.

———. "Happy Birthday, Ethel Waters." *Stereo Review* 37, no. 4 (October, 1976), 119.

Reed, Bill. *Hot from Harlem: Profiles in Classic African-American Entertainment*. Los Angeles: Cellar Door, 1998.

Reitz, Rosetta. Liner notes for LP *Ethel Waters 1938–1939*. Rosetta Records, 1986.

Ricketts Sumner, Cid. *Quality*. New York: Bantam, 1947.

Rose, Al. *Eubie Blake*. New York: Schirmer, 1979.

Rose, Philip. *You Can't Do That on Broadway! A Raisin in the Sun and Other Theatrical Improbabilities*. New York: Limelight, 2001.

Rose, Phyllis. *Jazz Cleopatra: Josephine Baker in Her Time*. New York: Doublday, 1989.

Rye, Howard. "Visiting Firemen: Ethel Waters." *Storyville* 126 (August/September 1986), 218–22.

Sampson, Henry T. *Blacks in Blackface: A Source Book on Early Black Musical Shows*. London: Scarecrow Press, 1980.

———. *Blacks in Black and White: A Source Book on Black Films* (2nd ed.). London: Scarecrow Press, 1995.

———. *Swingin' on the Etherwaves: A Chronological History of African Americans in Radio and Television Broadcasting, 1925–1955* (Vol. 1 and 2). Lanham, Md.: Scarecrow Press, 2005.

Schickel, Richard. *Elia Kazan: A Biography*. New York: HarperCollins, 2005.

Shaw, Arnold. *Black Popular Music in America*. New York: Schirmer, 1986.

———. *The Jazz Age: Popular Music in the 1920s*. New York: Oxford University Press, 1987.

Singer, Barry. *Black and Blue: The Life and Lyrics of Andy Razaf*. New York: Schirmer, 1992.

Smith, Mona Z. *Becoming Something: The Story of Canada Lee*. New York: Faber and Faber, 2004.

Spencer Carr, Virginia. *The Lonely Hunter: A Biography of Carson McCullers*. New York: Doubleday, 1975.

Stanfield, Peter. *Body and Soul: Jazz and Blues in American Film 1927–63*. Urbana: University of Illinois Press, 2005.

Stearns, Marshall, and Jean Stearns. *Jazz Dance: The Story of American Vernacular Dance*. New York: Macmillan, 1968.

Stewart-Baxter, Derrick. *Ma Rainey and the Classic Blues Singers*. London: November Books, 1970.

Stott, William, and Jane Stott. *On Broadway*. London: Thames and Hudson, 1979.

Summers, Claude J., ed. *The Queer Encyclopedia of Film and Television*. San Francisco: Cleis Press, 2005.

Taylor, Frank C., and Gerald Cook. *Alberta Hunter: A Celebration in Blues*. New York: McGraw-Hill, 1987.

Thompson, Leslie, and Jeffrey Green. *Leslie Thompson: An Autobiography*. Crawley, U.K.: Rabbit Press, 1985.

Vincent, Ted. *Keep Cool: The Black Activists Who Built the Jazz Age*. London: Pluto Press, 1995.

Waters, Ethel. *To Me It's Wonderful*. New York: Harper and Row, 1972.

Waters, Ethel, with Charles Samuels. *His Eye Is on the Sparrow*. London: Allen, 1951. Reprint, New York: Da Capo, 1992.

Watkins, Mel. *On the Real Side: A History of African American Comedy from Slavery to Chris Rock* (Rev. ed.). New York: Simon and Schuster, 1999.

Watts, Jill. *Hattie McDaniel: Black Ambition, White Hollywood*. New York: Amistad, 2005.

Woll, Allen. *Black Musical Theatre: From Coontown to Dreamgirls*. Baton Rouge: Louisiana State University Press, 1989.

Young, Jeff. *Kazan on Kazan*. London: Faber and Faber, 1999.

Zinnemann, Fred. *Fred Zinnemann: An Autobiography*. London: Bloomsbury, 1992.

Index

Names

Adams, Mark, xx
Adams, Maud, 44
Aldridge, Amanda Ira, 23
Aldridge, Ira, 23
Alexander, Michael, 66
Anderson, Eddie "Rochester," x, xiii,
    48, 51–52, 58, 60–62
Anderson, Edith (Ching), 2–4
Anderson, Ernest, 71
Anderson, Ivie, 36
Anderson, Judith, 45, 65
Anderson, Lewis (Louis), 1–2, 5
Anderson, Louise, 1–5
Anderson, Marian, viii, 22–23, 43, 50,
    118
Anderson, Sarah (Sally), 1–2, 4–5, 74, 82
Anderson, Viola (Vi), 2–5
Andrew, Geoff, 55
Andrews, Julie, xi, 54
Archer, Osceola, 90
Arlen, Harold, 33–34, 51, 53, 62, 120
Armstrong, Louis, x–xi, xii–xiii, 50–51,
    125

Arthur, Jean, 54
Aschenbrenner, Joyce, 48
Astaire, Fred, 98–99
Atkinson, Brooks, 45, 48, 81
Ayler, Ethel, 118

Bacall, Lauren, 94
Bagnold, Enid, 42
Bailey, Charles P., 8
Bailey, Mildred, xi
Bailey, Pearl, 85, 97, 109
Baker, Josephine, vii, ix, 11–13, 16, 22,
    27, 41, 50, 88, 123
Balanchine, George, 48
Baldwin, James, 60, 105
Ball, Lucille, 54
Bankhead, Tallulah, 31, 45, 63
Barnes, Ken, 124
Barrett, Mary Ellin, 41
Barrios, Richard, 17
Barrows, Cliff, 104
Barrymore, Ethel, 44, 74–75, 77, 81–82,
    121
Basie, Count, 63
Baskette, James, 71, 77

Theatre

Television

Radio

Songs

~

About the Author

Stephen Bourne (who is proud to share his birthday with Ethel Waters: October 31) is one of Britain's leading authorities on black history. He is the author of *Aunt Esther's Story* (1996, a biography of his aunt, a black seamstress born in London before the First World War), *A Ship and a Prayer* (1999), *Black in the British Frame: The Black Experience in British Film and Television* (second edition, 2001), *Sophisticated Lady: A Celebration of Adelaide Hall* (2001), *Elisabeth Welch: Soft Lights and Sweet Music* (2005), and *Speak of Me as I Am: The Black Presence in Southwark Since 1600* (2005). Stephen is currently working on *Remembering Butterfly McQueen*, his third book for Scarecrow Press. He has coresearched *100 Black Screen Icons*, a website for Every Generation and the British Film Institute. He has organized many film and television events for the National Film Theatre in London, including retrospectives dedicated to the careers of Ethel Waters (1993), Elisabeth Welch (1994), Anna May Wong (1995), and Paul Robeson (1998). For British television he was a researcher on Channel 4's *Sophisticated Lady* (1989, a profile of Adelaide Hall), Channel 4's *We Sing and We Dance* (1992, a profile of the Nicholas Brothers), and BBC-2's *Black and White in Colour* (1992, a two-part history of black people in British television). For the BBC's Windrush season in 1998, he researched and scripted Radio 2's *Their Long Voyage Home*. Stephen has been interviewed in several documentaries, including Channel 4's *Black Divas* (1996), BBC-2's *Black Britain* (1997), and *Paul Robeson: Here I Stand* (1999, an *American Masters* presentation). In 2007 Stephen was interviewed by the Criterion Collection for their special edition DVD box set of Paul Robeson's films. Stephen has received two Race in the Media awards from the Commission for Racial Equality, and for *Black in the British Frame* he was short-listed for *The Voice* newspaper's Black Community Award for Literature. In 1988 Stephen graduated from the London College of Printing with a bachelor of arts honors degree in film and television, and in 2006 he was awarded a master's of philosophy (MPhil) degree from De Montfort University in Leicester.